# Real Estate Careers

Also by the authors

*All America's Real Estate Book*

# Real Estate Careers

## 25 Growing Opportunities

**Carolyn Janik and Ruth Rejnis**

John Wiley & Sons, Inc.

New York • Chichester • Brisbane • Toronto • Singapore

*Library of Congress Cataloging-in-Publication Data:*

Janik, Carolyn.
    Real estate careers: 25 growing opportunities
/ Carolyn Janik and Ruth Rejnis.
        p.   cm.
    Includes bibliographical references.
    ISBN 0-471-59204-8.—ISBN 0-471-59203-X (pbk.)
    1. Real estate business—Vocational guidance.   I. Rejnis, Ruth.
II. Title.
HD1375.035   1994
333.33'023'73—dc20                                                        93-8279

Printed in the United States of America

10 9 8 7 6 5 4 3 2 1

For our brothers

Leo Lech
and
John Rejnis

# Contents

# Preface

Why real estate? Maybe you *know* you're not right for sales, and real estate is sales, right?

Wrong! Well, partly wrong.

Real estate is one of the largest industries in the United States. Think about it. Your home, your workplace, and your recreation and vacation places, they're all real estate. Nothing touches a more diverse spectrum of human needs than the land and everything attached to it.

The image of the real estate industry may be defined by the work of its salespeople, but that image is supported by the work of people with almost every type of personality and an array of talents. Within the industry, there are many, many jobs, and the skill sets required are both diverse and often overlapping. As you might expect, people often move from one career to another, building upon acquired skills while developing their individual talents.

In an industry so large and so diverse, however, few people really know the many available career paths and the appropriate stops along the way. So we've written a book to introduce you to some of the possibilities in the real estate world. Think of it as a VIP, behind-the-scenes tour of a huge industrial park. We'll take you down the roads, drive by and talk about some of the buildings, stop in at others, open some doors, and introduce you to some key people.

Each of the careers in this real estate industry park merits a book of its own (in fact, many have already been written), but before you delve into the nuts and bolts of a specialty, you will certainly want an overview. That is our goal: to give you both the perspective of distance and some close-up insights of workaday knowledge. With that in mind, we explain the first ten career choices in depth and provide a general overview of another 15 opportunities.

All the stories and quotations you will read here are from real people who spoke with us during nine months of extensive, nationwide interviewing. In a small number of instances, however, names and identifying data have been changed or withheld at the request of the participants in order to allow them to speak more freely while maintaining their privacy.

In addition to the perspectives and insights gathered from our research, we've also provided you with a sampling of other information sources at the end of most chapters and in the three appendixes. Please bear in mind, however, that these listings are only the whiskers on the cat. You would probably need a back-pack to carry a complete listing of real estate source material. Rather than weigh you down with everything for everyone, we hope that the suggested sources will lead you to others as you focus your questions and your goals.

We hope that this book will open the door to the proverbial "big break" for you. That's what it can do—open doors and give you a glimpse of what's inside. Beyond that, you must go on your own. The work of seizing an opportunity or grasping the significance of an insight and then developing that advantage into a fulfilling and successful career is yours. Go for it! We wish you all the very best.

CAROLYN JANIK
RUTH REJNIS

# PART I | Ten Careers in Depth

| CHAPTER

1 | # What's Developing?

*Subdivisions, Shopping Centers, Urban Renewal, Resorts . . .*

A developer is a person who can look at a piece of empty land and imagine it with buildings, roads, and landscaping. He or she might see single-family houses, condominiums or apartment buildings, a shopping center, an industrial park, or an office complex. A recreational developer can look at a dilapidated farm and see a five-star resort. An urban developer can look at a city's grime-and-crime area and see South Street Seaport or Larimer Square.

But so can a dreamer. What differentiates the developer from the dreamer is the knowledge and perseverance to get the work done. This is a career for the risk-taker who is very, very careful.

## The Work

Developers don't do any work. Well, not pick-and-shovel work anyway. And not task-oriented work either. This career calls for strategic planning, problem solving, and creativity. It demands the kind of high-stress, long-hours mental work that drives many of its professionals to take up jogging for exercise and meditation for relaxation. Successful practitioners, however, might exercise and meditate on their yachts in the Caribbean.

The work in *every* developer's *every* undertaking begins with site and project selection. If a developer owns a piece of land or an option on a piece of land, he or she must find the project that would put that land to its highest and best use. If the developer has a project in mind, then he or she must find the land that will best facilitate the realization of that project.

Some beginning developers do the first steps of this hunting and planning work themselves. Soon, however, other profession-

3

als are inevitably called in to do feasibility studies, building design, land-use design, site preparation studies, and financing. Choosing these professionals is an important part of the developer's work because the quality of their advice will affect his or her chances of success.

Because land use in any given municipality is governed by zoning ordinances and the community's master plan, a developer often spends a great deal of time and considerable money preparing an application for planning board approval. Because protocol is strict and red tape abundant even in the smallest towns and for the smallest projects, most developers use the services of a local lawyer to get them through the process. Setbacks and delays are common, and local politics are almost always a factor.

Financing is another prerequisite to development. Getting it is usually the beginning developer's highest hurdle. The preparation necessary to approach a commercial bank can require weeks of work. Remember, we're not talking about a simple home mortgage application here. An application for construction financing usually includes a formal written proposal that describes the project, its schedule, its costs, and its expected returns. Often, a professional feasibility study is attached. After the developer presents the proposal, the lender's consideration process starts. Meetings, negotiations, and approvals can consume many additional weeks.

Rather than approach lending institutions in person, some developers call upon the income property finance specialist of a local mortgage broker to help find appropriate financing. In other situations, a joint venture with a mortgage banker will be arranged. Sometimes a developer will approach an individual investor, asking that person to act as a silent partner, one who will provide the financing and share the profits without assuming any responsibility for supervising the project. (Not infrequently, the novice developer's first silent partner is a parent or other relative.) With larger projects, sometimes lawyers are called in to create limited partnerships, and then marketing specialists are hired to sell shares to raise the necessary capital.

Once the site is selected, the project designed, the municipal planning board's approval obtained, and the financing arranged, the developer usually hires a contractor to supervise the actual construction. Then, if there's no other project in the works, the developer might take a vacation. It's usually a short one, however. Six months in Tahiti is rarely a possibility because there are *always* problems during the construction process, and the buck *always* stops at the developer's desk.

Sometime during the development process, often pre-construction, the sales or leasing process is implemented. Here again, the developer usually hires professionals to prepare the marketing material and to sell or lease the proposed units or space. In commercial developments, preleasing is common and sometimes essential to the undertaking. In residential developments, sales efforts often begin even before a model home can be completed. As space, units, houses, or buildings are sold or leased, each contract is brought to the developer or his or her representative.

Some developers, especially residential developers, sell all the units they create and move on to other projects. Developers of commercial or recreational property, however, often lease space in their structures and continue to own and manage their projects, often by hiring management specialists (such as a shopping center manager or an apartment building superintendent) who report directly to the development company.

*Boring* is not a word in the developer's vocabulary. The work is varied, often stressful, and sometimes very exciting. Dana Crawford, of Urban Neighborhoods in Denver, Colorado, has been developing properties since the mid-1960s. Although she has worked on more than 40 urban developments in many parts of the United States, she still sees getting the financing as the most difficult part of the job.

When asked "What's the best part?" however, her answer is immediate. "When the lights go on!"

## The Money

The scene is a family dining table at the parents' retirement condo in Scottsdale, Arizona. It's spring break time, and two of the five adult children are visiting. We hear one brother, a man of about 45, talking.

"This looks like a great year for me," he says. "I made four million dollars last month."

No, he didn't win the lottery. That's the way it is when you're a major developer. There are no weekly or monthly paychecks. In fact, in the early stages of your career, you may never know when your next check is coming. When checks do arrive, however, they are often very substantial indeed.

But there's a flip side: *The risks are just as substantial.* This is a business in which things unknown inevitably affect outcome and everything takes longer than scheduled. Developers must wait many months, sometimes years, for invested money to bring a return. Success is often dependent on factors beyond the developer's control. And failure can lead to bankruptcy.

"Is there no middle ground?" you ask. "No way to begin earning money as a developer while maintaining some financial security?"

Well, yes. Many an aspiring developer begins his or her first small project as a part-time venture, keeping a full-time job until the project's successful completion brings in some capital and establishes a track record that will help in obtaining financing for future projects.

The person who buys a house on an oversized lot, subdivides the property, and has another house built on the newly created lot is a developer. So is the person who buys a big rundown, nineteenth-century house at auction and converts it into a multifamily house or a three-unit condominium. And also the person who pays $500 to buy a $60,000 option on a trash-laden corner lot, does a feasibility study, and then sells the lot to Exxon at $250,000. Each of these and many other development projects can be done while holding down a full-time job.

Later in their careers, many developers build properties that can be leased and will bring in a solid income base of regular monthly payments. New projects are then structured so that failure cannot affect the ownership of and income from the existing projects.

Other experienced developers work for development companies that function as development managers for major institutions (banks, corporations, foreign investors, and so on). In this arrangement, the developer works for a fee plus a percentage of the profits (usually 10 to 15 percent). The risk of loss is on the institution that hires the developer. With the eliminated risk, however, the developer's potential profit becomes limited.

Some young would-be developers seek task or project management jobs with large, well-established developers. Robert Miller, executive vice-president and general manager of Marriott Ownership Resorts in Lakeland, Florida, and the developer of Marriott's Cypress Harbour in Orlando, had a staff of three working on the

500-unit ownership resort development for five years. Salaries of these professionals were not available, but Miller estimates that entry-level compensation is in the $30,000 to $50,000 range with wide variation.

Because developing real estate is one of the most lucrative careers available to entrepreneurial North Americans, success can bring fame as well as fortune. Virtually everyone recognizes names like Donald Trump and Bill Marriott, for example. On the other hand, there are many, many other developers with similar fortunes who have chosen to maintain a lower profile and limit their "fame" to local restaurants and country clubs.

While holding out this promise of riches and fame, the career also has a dark side potential. There are thousands of stories associated with the S&L bailout that illustrate the possibilities of mismanagement and even fraud. One of the most talked about occurred in Connecticut.

On March 9, 1992, the *New York Times* ran a full-page story about Jonathan Googel and Benjamin Sisti, founders of Colonial Realty Company. Their life-style had been fabulous, and their wealth had seemed immense. On the front page of the newspaper was a photo of Sisti's 52,000-square-foot home. It was in foreclosure and about to be auctioned.

Almost 6,000 people had invested more than $350 million in Colonial's limited partnerships, and most of them were screaming fraud and mismanagement. Banks had foreclosed on a pyramid of loans and forced Colonial into bankruptcy. Not only was the company bankrupt, however, the principals were also under federal investigation. In the end, the economy of an entire state was negatively affected by the failures of this development company.

## The People

Advisers, suppliers, supervisors, investors, employees, and customers—these are the people in a developer's business life. Interactions with them will determine his or her degree of success.

"Not true!" you say. "What about money, land, and luck?"

Luck, yes, that's a factor. But luck can be courted by good management. Money and land? Acquisition of both is dependent on other people in the real estate marketplace. Let's look at how.

Risk will destroy a developer who operates without professional *advisers* or with poor ones. The transfer of real estate is a process governed by contracts and laws, and a lawyer is essential. Tax laws regarding real estate development are a multilayered web on the local, state, and federal levels, and no developer should operate without an accountant. Real estate counselors are often called in to do feasibility studies. Architects are necessary to design buildings. Site and environmental specialists are needed to advise on land preparation.

You may be thinking of *suppliers* as the people who deliver bricks and mortar. And of course that's right, every developer must deal with materials wholesalers. But think of suppliers in a broader sense. Suppliers of money, for example. A developer must deal with lenders again and again. And how about suppliers of land? A developer must be enough of a negotiator to convince landowners to sell at an acceptable price.

When you're working as a developer, the concept of *supervisors* has little relation to the word "boss." Municipal authorities—usually the planning board, the buildings department, and the environmental protection department—become de facto supervisors of the project. A developer cannot proceed without their approvals.

*Investors* enable many projects to come into being. Sometimes they are the stockholders of banks or lending institutions, sometimes joint venture partners, and sometimes the shareholders in a limited partnership. In each case, the developer has made the investors a promise in return for the use of their money. Satisfaction is demanded.

As you might expect, a large developer has *employees* with many different occupations. But so does even the smallest developer. Just imagine yourself creating a simple one-house subdivision and you will see yourself as an employer of carpenters, plumbers, roofers, surveyors, real estate agents, and more. How well you choose and supervise the people who work for you will be another determining factor in your success.

And finally, *customers*. A developer doesn't make any money until a property is sold or leased. When selling residential property, marketing to attract customers is essential, and specialists are often hired to create a marketing plan. When selling or leasing commercial property, the developer often meets the prospective customers or their representatives personally. Lunch, dinner, and golf dates are common.

People management (in the widest possible sense of the term) is just as important to the career of a successful developer as risk management. People make the development process happen and, ideally, the process happens for the benefit of people. The developer, therefore, must possess excellent interactive skills.

## Getting In

Twenty years ago, Al Kainer started a project in New Jersey with a piece of land, a dump truck without brakes, and a partner who knew about as little as he did. By trial and error and through long hours that often stretched far into the night, the two men worked out the problems of planning a residential community on land with poor drainage. They finally got subdivision approval for seven lots. Before they could put their ancient dump truck to use, however, a builder came along and made them an offer they couldn't refuse. They had turned a $20,000 investment into $130,000 in six months.

Would you call Kainer a developer? You could. Unlike lawyers, there are no bar exams for developers. Not everyone, however, starts off with a dream and a prayer. There are educational opportunities that can diminish the risks, the mistakes, and the hours of searching for answers. The Massachusetts Institute of Technology, the University of Wisconsin, and the Urban Land Institute all offer specialized programs in development. In addition, 40 colleges in the United States offer degree programs in real estate. Thirty have master's programs, and six offer the doctorate. To learn how to get more information, see Appendix II.

Some undergraduates and recent graduates get started by using options or by subdividing oversized lots or small tracts of land. Few, however, are able to overcome the huge obstacle that prevents novice developers from embarking independently on a major project: financing. It's virtually impossible to get major project financing without some professional experience and a good track record.

Because it's generally agreed that a job with a well-established developer is the safest and easiest way to get the needed experience and build some business connections while doing so, many recent graduates with a major in real estate send out résumés and fill out application forms. But this career path is not without problems. Entry-level jobs are scarce, and those fortunate enough to land one are usually assigned a specialized function, such as materials supervision or site preparation supervision. These successful employees become proficient in their specialized functions, but they do not learn the broad spectrum of skills necessary to a career as an independent developer. To learn the business through the corporate route, therefore, the aspiring developer must move from position to position and sometimes from employer to employer for a number of years.

But what if your résumé brings only rejection letters? For young men and women determined to break in even though all doors seem shut, Carl Burlingame, editor and publisher of *Resort Development and Operation*, recommends joining the sales force at one of the big interval-ownership resorts (time-share developments). "This is performance-oriented commission work," he says, "but it does give you a chance to get a foot in the door."

For those who are still in college, the International Foundation for Timesharing (IFT) has a limited number of summer intern programs available. Students work at time-share resorts in marketing and sales, property management, development and financing, or hospitality. For more information, contact IFT at the American Resort and Residential Development Association (ARRDA), which is listed in Appendix I.

Among the established careers that are abandoned in favor of becoming a developer, real estate finance probably ranks first. Because they have experience in what most developers refer to as "the hardest part of the job" (getting the money), some mortgage brokers and mortgage bankers feel qualified to take on the whole job. The motivation, of course, is usually the expectation of collecting the whole profit pie.

When an opportunity presents itself, some real estate sales agents and brokers, especially those who work extensively in commercial, industrial, or land sales, also change careers and enter developing. These people usually have well-stocked "warehouses" of knowledge and business connections. Their experience and their networks give them the confidence and often open the doors to the financial backing necessary to venture into major project development. Similar experience and connections enable some men and women in the construction industry, some urban planners, and some municipal buildings inspection department officials to make the same career move.

When lawyers become developers, it is usually as silent

partners in joint ventures. It's difficult for most lawyers to be silent for very long, however, and many get involved in their projects. Some of them like the work and its rewards and give up general practice to take on major projects, either alone or with a group.

No matter what a person's background, the requirement for intimate knowledge of real estate in *all* its aspects is a formidable barrier to becoming a developer. To break through that barrier, you can choose a small project and learn some aspects of the job with every step you take, or you can work on one particular aspect of a large project and observe the rest of the process very carefully.

## Is This for You?

Would you like to be rich? That's a good start. But to join the ranks of successful (and rich) developers, you must also be willing to take risks—big ones. A string of zeros after the first digit next to the dollar sign can't scare you off. Nor can the complexity of a project and its immense time and money requirements.

Developing a piece of property is in some ways like doing a jigsaw puzzle. Whether the project has 500 or 5,000 pieces, you must be willing to separate and organize the parts, work various segments concurrently, and then bring everything together to form a whole. If you are overwhelmed by the many parts of the job or if you get hung up on one difficult part and can't work around it, you won't finish. So, like the puzzle-maker, the developer needs patience, perseverance, flexibility, and a keen eye for detail.

A developer must also have a strong ego and enough self-confidence to believe that he or she can accomplish a goal when other people are shaking their heads. He or she must be willing to take on difficult problems and come up with creative solutions. He or she must be a team leader as well as an executive who takes responsibility for what is being done. And always, a developer must see the possibilities while anticipating the problems.

Richard Mulvaney, a developer in Massachusetts, recently said, "You know, banks have a prioritized list of good lending risks, and right now developers are at the bottom."

You might ask, "Why? Is it all problems right now? Is there no positive outlook for being a developer?"

The answer is yes and no. New England was among the areas worst hit by the early 90's economic downturn, and you can't really blame the banks for being ultracautious. There and in other areas of the country, many types of construction are overbuilt. Developers have put up too many office buildings, too many condominiums, or too many high-priced single-family homes.

However, according to the Urban Land Institute's book, *Professional Real Estate Development* by Richard B. Peiser with Dean Schwanke, 1992 was the bottom of a 50-year cycle, and the movement will be upward from there. The career outlook is positive for those who carefully research the needs of an area and its population group and fill those needs.

Currently, demographics predict increasing demand for vacation and retirement homes, long-term health-care facilities, apartment buildings, small homes, and urban renewal projects. But demographic predictions change, as do commercial and industrial needs, and the astute developer will be aware of both the predictions and the possibilities for new directions.

Is this for you? You may not be able to tell until you try it, but we'd like you to hold onto one thought if you venture into this career. Whether you begin by joining a huge development company or by subdividing a lot to build one extra house, remember that the worst developers leave trails of ugliness and financial disaster, whereas the best make the world a little better.

## For More Information

ARRDA's prospective members kit includes a copy of the Code of Standards and Ethics, a list of publications, and a list of audiotapes available to the public.

The Urban Land Institute (ULI) offers workshops, seminars, and a variety of publications. An excellent guide to establishing a career in the five major types of development (land subdivision, multifamily residential, office, industrial, and retail) is *Professional Real Estate Development: The ULI Guide to the Business*, by Richard B. Peiser with Dean Schwanke (Chicago: Dearborn Financial Publishing and the Urban Land Institute, 1992).

# Buying and Rehabbing Houses and Apartment Buildings

It is a dream shared by many investors, and more than one average homeowner: I'll buy a somewhat run-down house, fix it up, and then sell it—at a sizable profit, of course. Or, better yet, I'll rent it and then buy another and rent that, and pretty soon I'll own 20 houses and I'll be rich!

Those daydreams. What would life be without them? "But it has been done," you say. Yes, indeed, it was done very successfully in the 1970s and 1980s, when property appreciated at sometimes double digits annually, shortening the road to real estate riches. Let's take a look at today's rehab market. Can you make a full-time career of fixing up houses, or will it more likely be an avocation or hobby?

## The Work

You are not likely to be interested in this particular real estate arena if you do not already have an eye for seeing the worn, shabby house as an investment opportunity. Most buyers look for a little cream puff of a place, but *you* see that behind the chipped paint, overgrown shrubbery, clutter, and old-fashioned touches is a little gem that can be dusted off to become your ticket to wealth.

There is far more to developing smarts in the rehab business than these few paragraphs allow. Books are written on the subject (some excellent ones are recommended at the end of this chapter). Still, this chapter can discuss the major points in this career/avocation. They might cheer you on in your already sound thinking or hand you a dose of cold reality about this seemingly easy-to-handle realty specialty.

Here are some highlights of what a rehabber should look for—and watch out for—suggested by those who have made the fix-up business work for them.

You must know your community well. You should only think of investing in the area in which you now live or within a few miles of home. David T. Schumacher, author of *The Buy and Hold Real Estate Strategy* (see "For More Information") and an investor in California real estate that has brought him millions of dollars during his 30 years in the business, says, "When I first started out in this, I wouldn't buy anything I couldn't ride my bicycle to."

Knowing your community means reading the entire daily newspaper, not just the real estate section. You should also attend city council meetings so you will learn what is planned for the town, what the problems are and whether they are likely to be remedied, and any number of other news nuggets that, when put together, present a complete profile of your particular investment climate.

You need to talk to people too: the folks in the council chambers as well as the man or woman on the street. Notice where the "For Sale" signs are springing up and how long it takes for them to be converted to "Sold."

You will probably have to take on all of this without the help of a support group. There is no real national association composed of investors of this type, although there may be some regional groups. Your guides will be books and other people's experiences.

Not so incidentally, we are talking about houses for investment here, not townhomes or condominiums, which yield little if any profit in this enterprise.

Do not forget that magic real estate formula: Location is everything. If the property you are eyeing is in a good neighborhood, you will always be able to sell it because there will always be an interested buyer. There is an exception—or at least a qualification—to this rule. Many neighborhoods around the country are experiencing a rebirth, thanks to house-hunters who seek affordable housing and to bring homes of architectural or historic note back to their former good looks. Some of those blocks may not look so great now, but the move toward rehabilitation and renovation has begun, and they present an excellent opportunity for the rehabber who, after considerable research, sees that this is indeed a perfect opportunity to get in on the ground floor of an investment certain to go up, up, up.

You have to be careful here, though. The wiser buys are in a community where about one-quarter of the houses have been rehabilitated or are in varying stages of fix-up. If there are too few of those homes, the renaissance may die on the vine. If there are too many, you are probably going to be priced out of an affordable purchase.

From all of your research, you will of course know where the toxic waste sites are in your locale, whether a filling station is planned next to the house, and similar disadvantages to an investment purchase. Location does not have to mean just a certain part of town, either. It can zero in on a particular house within a layout of streets.

Keep in constant touch with real estate agents in your area so that you do not miss anything of note, including gossip about the market, new listings, and trends. Schmooze all you can!

Decide whether you want to enter into this investment alone or with a partner, even a team, to help you. Do you have any talent in the area of fixing up houses? If you cannot do at least some of the work yourself, it will be costly to hire professionals all along the way. They will cut deeply into your profit when you sell, especially if you are aiming for a relatively fast turnover. Many who choose rehabbing bring in a partner who is skilled in some of the trades. Perhaps you have all the skills but need some financing. That could be your reason for seeking a partner or two. Another viable scenario is for the lone investor to have some skills, doing much work alone and farming out major projects.

Know how much capital you will need and where that money will come from. You will need some money of your own for this new sideline. Are you stretched thin with a mortgage, home equity loan, and kids nearing college age? Perhaps this is an argument for taking in a partner who can provide some financing.

Know your lending community. In other words, make friends with your banker after doing some homework to see which is indeed the best, most welcoming institution for your purposes. What is the thinking in your financial community right now, especially about real estate investment? Is there a drift toward even more conservatism than usual for bankers? Or are things pretty solid now, with lenders unloosening the purse strings a bit?

Mortgage qualification standards have been tightened up in recent years for a number of reasons. With today's tougher lending rules, you may find it harder to secure financing and so might your expected buyers. It will pay you to thoroughly learn the financing ropes, a point that becomes even more important if you anticipate problems.

You will want to check "comparables," or "comps," before buying anything. Those, of course, are what other homes in the neighborhood have recently brought their sellers. You will get a good idea of what you should be paying for your purchase. Comps are available at real estate sales offices.

It is vitally important to know what constitutes a good buy in a rehab house. A good buy is a dwelling that is structurally sound, no matter what else is wrong with it. Skip the homes with serious termite damage, major structural problems, or dry rot. Other problems you can handle. "In buying houses 40 or more years old," says rehabber Billy Lewis, "you have to remember people were not that concerned with termites back then, and they often didn't use proper foundations because either there were no building codes at all or they were not as strong as they are now." Lewis has renovated or restored several houses, some dating to the early nineteenth century, in Quincy, Florida, a small town near Tallahassee that has an attractive historic district in its center. Lewis adds that level, even floors and walls are another necessity in considering the purchase of an old house. "You have to be sure that the house will meet the standards of the lending institution where a buyer applies for a mortgage," Lewis adds. "The lender will inspect it."

A new roof for an old house is costly, but no more so than upgrading a 1940s kitchen, and neither should be considered serious deterrents to an otherwise viable purchase. It is best to try for the house that can use some minor construction and repair work but whose main problem is that it is drab. Those are the homes that can be "charmed up" with small upgrades, paint, wallpaper, some interior architectural details, and improved landscaping. Know the difference between repairing and improving, too. Repairs will be expected by the buyer, who will not pay more for them. Improving casts the house in a new, favorable light, attracting buyers who are willing to pay higher prices.

It is not wise to overimprove for the particular neighborhood. "You don't put bidets in working-class neighborhood houses," says Sandra M. Brassfield, author of *Profiting from Real Estate Rehab*. Brassfield has spent 15 years in lending, with an emphasis on neighborhood revitalization, and has completed some 32 rehab projects.

Work the numbers on any property that seriously interests you. "Ideally, in a perfect world, we try to get $2 of return for every $1 of rehabilitation," Brassfield explains. "If you get $1.50 back, the thing to remember is that the aggregate is greater than the individual components. If you pick the right property to improve, the sum total of your having done the right things is going to add up to more than 150 percent return on some items."

Be careful when buying a historic house or one that is situated in a historic district, whether it is on a local, state, or federal historic registry. You could have no control over some changes you will want to make to that property.

There is another consideration regarding historic homes. Lewis points out that it is unrealistic to buy an old house that needs work and then spend, spend, spend to bring it back to its original splendor *and* expect to make a neat little profit when you sell. (An exception here might be a home in a very hot revival neighborhood, but even there the cost of purchasing a shell is likely to be substantial, let alone spending another $200,000—or more—for restoration.) Will someone be willing to pay the hundreds of thousands of dollars your fixer-upper has cost you, plus what you hope to realize as profit? Work the numbers carefully.

Lewis works on his own properties and on houses for residents in and around Quincy, many of whom hire him for authentic restorations of very handsome houses. Naturally, these days it is not possible to be *totally* authentic. First, some materials are just not available anymore or are prohibitively expensive. Second, an authentic eighteenth-century house would have no central heat or air and no indoor plumbing! Most of us are willing to carry "authentic restoration" only so far.

"I personally bought a 1918 Sears package home," Lewis explains. "I anticipate making a profit because I'm having only *some* custom-made details." He adds, "You can't make that kind of house too modern either, of course."

Despite the caveats, historic districts have a cachet with buyers. The secret, of course, is to buy that interesting house at a low or at least reasonable price and to balance carefully the amount of money you spend fixing it up for resale.

Another consideration is whether you want to sell the house quickly or hold it for a few years. Some rehabbers believe that you should make the fix-ups as quickly as you can, sell for the highest price you can get—in a good market, of course—pocket the profit, and then move on to the next purchase.

Schumacher, whose background in Southern California includes many years spent as an appraiser, holds the opposite view, as might be expected from the title of his book. "I recommend that you buy and hold for a long period of time," he says, "so that you take advantage of the growth pattern there. People who buy and sell after one or two years miss the big profit." Indeed, frequent house flipping might not work well these days, with property values rising almost infinitesimally, if at all, in some areas of the country.

Which is the better policy? There are arguments for both sides, and much depends on the neighborhood you have chosen and its likely growth path. Another consideration is your personal situation. Can you afford, financially and otherwise, to carry several properties for quite a few years? The reading and research you will do before making your first investment will help crystallize your expectations from your investment venture.

A few words about buying small apartment buildings are in order. It is best to start—and probably stay—small. Schumacher and most others in the housing investment game feel that purchasing, say, two buildings of five units each is preferable to buying one ten-unit structure. "It takes more cash to buy the bigger one," Schumacher explains, "and you're dealing with a more sophisticated seller. Institutions are not interested in lending on the larger one because it doesn't have enough units to require a manager. People ought to try to buy a whole lot of small duplexes and triplexes around where they live and try to manage them themselves."

There are other concerns for those considering investing in a small apartment building. Rent control might keep rents prohibitively low. Landlord/tenant laws in your area might be stricter for owners of buildings above a certain number of units. This number varies according to town statutes but is usually around six. Finally, there might be so many new apartment complexes with all the bells and whistles and so many condominiums that can be rented that there will be little market for the older apartments that you will be trying to rent. If there *is* a demand for rental units, then think small, and you are apt to do quite well.

The final bit of advice is to read, read, read and study, study, study.

## The Money

To get back to the introduction to this chapter, can you make money in today's economy? Or, perhaps more accurately, can you make money in your community's current real estate market?

Brassfield suggests that rehabbing *can* be more than just a hobby. "Start part-time in the business," she directs, "with no more than two houses the first year. Get to the point where you would max out at three a year when you are still working full-time. You're not doing much hands-on work here, of course."

You *can* make a profit and even become quite wealthy from real estate wisely chosen and managed. Folks always have and probably always will. However, this is a delicate little dance you will have to do between knowing your community and its high and low points, choosing the right property at the right price, knowing the lenders' current rumblings in your town, and being able to read the minds of local sellers and then buyers for your properties.

## The People

To be a successful rehabber, you'll need assistance. You may have your cousin Fred to help with carpentry work, but that is not what we are talking about here. If you want to be professional about this—and how else will you be successful at it?—you will need a team comprising the following:

- A tax accountant. He or she can help you in decision making and warn you about pitfalls.
- A real estate attorney. You will confer with an attorney regularly if you are in a mortgage-issuing state, less often in a trust deed state, where escrow agents, not lawyers, handle house closings.
- A mortgage broker. You can read more about them in

Chapter 6, but for now here's a brief explanation of their work and how it will apply to you. Mortgage brokers market mortgages for banks, insurance companies, and other lenders. A broker will find a loan tailored for you, somewhere in this country, with some lender. He or she works on a percentage that is already worked into the loan. You will need this individual because you will sometimes be dealing with complicated purchase and rehabilitation loans or creative seller financing when you buy a rehabbing property or possibly when you are selling one. Mortgage brokers have access to every kind of lending available, and this one-stop shopping can save you time and frustration.

- A real estate agent. You will, of course, need an agent who knows the neighborhood you are considering for investment. We have talked about that in previous paragraphs.

- A general contractor. Last, but certainly not least, you might want to hook up with an able general contractor. Check around town if you do not already have your choice targeted. Some states have a licensing requirement for contractors that includes an exam; others allow anyone to paint his or her name on a panel truck after first securing a business license at city hall. You need someone who has an adequate supply of subcontractors, too. You will no doubt pick up a lot on your first job. In future purchases, you may be able to do yourself what you are paying some subcontractors for now.

   "Find a contractor doing houses on his own, and let him become your mentor," suggests Brassfield. "Maybe your choice would take in all of the usual requirements, but if you want to do rehabbing as a profession, go with one who knows how to choose real estate and one who has a good track record. The first time out, do whatever he wants you to do. Usually, you will have to supply some credit or cash. Essentially, you will be following him around like a puppy dog, learning a lot of tricks of the trade."

## Getting In

You will want to start small, perhaps gaining rehab experience by fixing up the house or apartment you live in now. You might also consider taking in a partner before you "officially" become a rehabber. As mentioned earlier, a partner could be a financial help or could supply hands-on skills. You should start looking around for your partner or team well before that first purchase.

In the best rehab situation, you find the house that seems ideal for your purposes and a seller who is willing to take little or no money down and who will arrange financing with you. If that is not the scenario for your sale, then of course you will head for a lender. Once you have that initial property, your equity in it can become the basis for a loan for acquiring and rehabbing more properties. Profits from sales are plowed back into still more purchases. With the buy-and-hold strategy, you will still have equity for loans and financing new projects until you ultimately sell.

## Is This for You?

After reading the above paragraphs, you probably know now whether this is an interest you should pursue or pass by, at least for now.

Schumacher says an important quality in a successful investor in this arena is friendliness. "This is a people business," he says. "Values are created by the actions and attitudes and thinking of people. If everybody thinks your house isn't worth a dime, then it isn't worth a dime. If they think it's worth $500,000, then it's worth $500,000. You have to change the attitude and thinking of people about your property and your community."

In this field, Brassfield notes, the perfectionist might have a tendency to overimprove and may never feel the property is ready for sale. On the other hand, someone who does not pay attention to detail will not likely be a success story either, she adds.

Here are some common pitfalls that even those past the neophyte stage can fall into: being too tight in making repairs and improvements in order to increase your profit if you plan a quick sale; trying to do too much yourself to save money when the work needed really calls for a professional; and not being organized in hiring and keeping track of your subcontractors.

If you do your homework as diligently as a student preparing for a final exam, you will no doubt avoid the major snags or will at least learn from the mistakes you do make. This will serve you well in your career—or sideline—as housing rehabber. Where you can make a little money, or a great deal of it.

## For More Information

*The Buy and Hold Real Estate Strategy*, by David T. Schumacher with Erick Page Bucy (New York: John Wiley & Sons, 1992) $29.95. The author advises real estate investors not to sell quickly, but instead to hold properties for the long term to accumulate equity that can be borrowed against to make other investments.

*Landlording*, by Leigh Robinson (El Cerrito, CA: Express Publishing, 1992) $21.95. Now in its sixth edition, this is practically a classic for the small landlord. It contains invaluable advice, checklists, sample management forms, and so on, and it is readable, even humorous, to boot.

*Profiting from Real Estate Rehab*, by Sandra M. Brassfield (New York: John Wiley & Sons, 1992) $19.95 paperback. A soup-to-nuts guide to finding, funding, rehabilitating, and marketing fixer properties.

The National Trust for Historic Preservation can help with information on rehabbing a house with architectural or historical significance or a house in a designated historic district. Write to the organization at 1785 Massachusetts Ave. NW, Washington, DC 20036, or call them at (202) 636-4514.

# CHAPTER 3

# "... And This Is the Living Room"

## Selling and Listing Residential Real Estate

It's a joke among experienced agents. They say that you can always tell a part-timer or a novice because he or she will say, "... and this is the living room." What else would a room with a formal sofa and chairs, a coffee table, matching end tables, cut glass lamps, and a fireplace be? And yet beginning agents consistently assume a tour guide persona, complete with Vanna White hand motions.

Why this unnatural posturing? Attitudes, probably. Many beginning agents operate from a perspective that reflects an inaccurate understanding of the career. For example, one of the most common snatches of conversation heard among women at license preparation school is, "I decided to go into real estate because I love looking at houses." Men, on the other hand, are more likely to get started because they think of themselves as powerfully persuasive salesmen—salesmen who have the know-how to point out the features while masking the faults.

What happens to these people? Well, there's a high dropout ratio. The National Association of Realtors (NAR) was unable to provide current statistics, but our informal survey confirmed that things haven't changed much from the NAR data published ten years ago, which showed that an estimated 40 percent of beginning real estate salespeople drop out of the business before the end of their first year and another 20 percent by the end of their second year. Less than 30 percent of any one group of beginners is still working in the field at the end of five years.

"Why do so many leave?" you ask.

Because this is a tough job where attitudes about checking out decorating and pumping up sales pressure work against success. Residential real estate sales has become a white-collar service profession. Professional training is required, and professional behavior is expected.

## The Work

State licensing laws refer to the man or woman working in the residential marketplace as a salesperson. In this job, however, there are two aspects to sales: selling and listing. A property is listed when homeowners sign a contract hiring an agency to act on their behalf in the sale of their home. Without listings, salespeople would have nothing to sell. For the real estate agent, therefore, it is just as important to "sell" homeowners on the services provided by the agency as it is to sell a home to prospective buyers.

The life of a residential salesperson requires the wearing of many hats. Although filling the roles symbolized by those various hats makes for interesting work, it also demands the development of a wide variety of skills, each of which must be well honed.

As a selling agent, you'll do work similar to that of a clerk, a tour guide, a financial adviser, a psychic, a salesperson, a negotiator, and an account manager. As a listing agent, you'll do work similar to that of a hunter/scout, appraiser, decorating consultant, marketing director, and therapist. Sounds like a lot, doesn't it? It is, and bear in mind that wearing all these hats is not a roleplaying exercise; these roles are the job. Let's look at them.

"Clerk!" you say. "Come on! Filing went out when computers came in."

Right, most information on shared listings is now distributed on computer-generated printouts. The hours that agents once spent updating their listing books can now be spent on the road. But the computer has not entirely eliminated the clerical work of this career. The required information on every listing must still be gathered in person and keyed into the Multiple Listing Service (MLS) computer system. Price changes and corrections must be recorded in office files and also reported to MLS. As a beginning agent (or whenever you change jobs to work for a new agency), you'll need time to familiarize yourself with the computer system being used in your office, and then you'll have to use it.

Besides the work involved in keeping MLS records up to date, files must be established and maintained on new customers, prospective customers, possible listing leads, and financing sources. In smaller agencies, you will also be required to answer the phone and act as receptionist during your scheduled "floor time"—that is, the hours during which you must be in the office so that any incoming business (prospective buyers or sellers) can be assigned to you.

Real estate agents become *tour guides* whenever they take customers (prospective buyers) out to inspect properties. As guides, they must be familiar with the properties being shown. It's no secret that top agents always preview a property before showing it to customers. Agents must also plan the route that will be traveled between showings, and they must call sellers to schedule appointments.

Many customers also ask their real estate agents to show them around town, which means pointing out schools, shopping areas, medical facilities, recreational areas, restaurants, bus and train stations, and child-care facilities. Agents often keep file drawers full of maps, brochures, and flyers to help acquaint newcomers with the communities being considered.

Before taking on the role of tour guide with a particular customer, however, a good agent will briefly act the part of a *financial adviser*. In the business, it's called "qualifying your buyer."

No agent wants to waste time showing properties that the customer can't afford, so qualifying is the standard practice of gathering personal financial information pertinent to the purchase of a home. Most often the actual calculations are now done by computer, but the agent must ask for information regarding available down payment, income, and debt. He or she then keys it in, reads the printouts, and advises customers as to how much monthly payment they can afford and how much house that will buy in various communities.

Later in the process, when the agent is acting in the role of negotiator, he or she may be required to give financial advice again. At that point, it's not only a question of affordability but also of property value, as compared to similar properties in the area.

"OK so far," you say, "but *psychic*? I haven't seen too many real estate agents with crystals hanging around their necks."

Well, maybe the word *is* a little much. But selling real estate does require a great deal of intuition and excellent listening skills. Often, what customers say they want is not really what they want. The best and most successful agents interpret reactions to properties being shown and then hone in on a property or selection of properties that is likely to appeal to the buyer.

Which brings us to the role of *salesperson*. In his autobiography, Lee Iacocca remembers being taught as a salesman to ask for the order, and the successful real estate agent must act likewise. It takes courage to ask for the first offer and even more courage to ask for signatures on a contract to purchase, especially if the buyers are anxious or defensive. Some franchise training programs teach their agents to use sales-peg lines such as, "Would you buy it if . . .?" Some brokers train their agents to get the buyers back to the office and begin writing up the deal "just to see how it looks."

Both techniques point up the role of the salesperson as facilitator. Because the process of home buying is anxiety ridden for most buyers, sales work for the agent usually means finding acceptable properties and then making the purchase as easy as possible. "Let me try this for you" is a line that starts many a buying process.

Playing the role of salesperson in a real estate transaction takes almost constant reevaluation of each situation and of the positions of the buyers and the sellers. Skillful agents know when to give a nudge, when to hold a hand, and when to pat a back.

These selling skills blend quite readily into those required as a *negotiator*, which is probably the make-or-break role for the majority of real estate careers. Most real estate agents don't get paid unless there's a "meeting of the minds" on price and contingencies, and there's rarely a meeting of the buyers' and sellers' minds without a good deal of negotiating. The negotiation process can last days or even weeks. It can run into the small hours of the morning. It can eat up an entire weekend. And it can cause many a sleepless night.

As a residential agent, you will both initiate and see through to completion or withdrawal all negotiations on offers from the buyers to whom you showed the property being sold. You might also be called into negotiations on a property that you listed if and when an offer is brought in by another agent. Whichever position you're in, you'll need plenty of patience, tact, perseverance, and most of all scrupulous honesty.

Once the deal has been made, the real estate agent becomes a kind of *account manager*. Between the handshakes-all-around stage and the passing of title from seller to buyer, there are a myriad of things to do and problems to solve and you, the agent, will be coordinator, complaint department, chief gofer, and more or less the person in charge. As the salesperson who brought in the buyer, you will help to arrange financing, keep after the lender to be sure the loan application is being attended to, keep after the buyer to be sure all necessary paperwork is submitted, arrange or help to arrange inspections and appraisals, answer innumerable questions, accompany buyers on their day-of-the-closing inspection, attend the closing, and collect the agency's commission check. As the salesperson who originally took the listing, you'll make sure the other agent is doing everything that should be done, or you'll do it yourself.

All these roles occupy the busy agent in a fast market, but what about work in a slow market or when you're just starting out? The agent in search of business is usually a *hunter* or *scout* on the trail of a listing. Among the tasks that residential specialists are required to do are cold canvass calling and "farming" (jargon for looking for listings). In cold canvass calling, you'll join the ranks of the telemarketers and neophyte stockbrokers who so often interrupt your dinner with the ring of the phone. Essentially, the agent calls every residence in an area, street by street, introduces him- or herself, and asks if the owner is planning a move in the near future. This same procedure is sometimes done by mail, with the envelopes hand-addressed and the letters signed in ink by the agent in search of business.

Farming is more personal and more time-consuming, but also, according to some agencies, more productive. Agents, either alone or in pairs, go from door to door throughout a neighborhood. Sometimes they give away calendars or kitchen gadgets as favors from the real estate office; always they introduce themselves and offer to set up an appointment to do a free competitive market analysis (CMA) of the value of the property.

When doing a CMA, the residential real estate agent is doing much the same work that an *appraiser* does. By using records of the sales of comparable properties in the area during the past year and by evaluating the size, structure, and condition of the property being inspected, the agent comes up with an estimated fair market value. In addition to predicting a probable selling price, the agent usually suggests an asking price. The dollar distance between the asking price and the probable selling price is usually determined by the tempo of the local marketplace.

To do a CMA or take a listing, an agent must inspect every room in a house, including the cellar, attic, and garage. In this part of the job, you may find yourself feeling a little like a *decorating consultant* as you answer the seller's questions and give advice on moving furniture, repapering, general cleanup, and what to put away (out of sight).

Once a listing contract is signed and the agency officially represents the seller, the listing agent puts on the hat of a *marketing director*. Newspaper advertisements must be budgeted and copy written, photos taken, brochures printed, and open houses scheduled and sat through. Some agencies now make videotapes of the exterior and interior of every listing, using the tapes as in-office previews for agents and customers. Occasionally, listing agents do these tapings themselves, but most offices schedule professionals for the job.

The listing agent is also responsible for having the sign placed on the property and sending "We've just listed your neighbor's home" letters to every home in a radius of several blocks. (Some of the quickest sales are to the friends of neighbors.)

Finally, the residential salesperson inevitably becomes a pseudo*therapist* if a listed home does not sell within the expected time frame. The anxiety of home sellers is even worse than that of home buyers because they usually have the greater part of their life savings tied up in equity. In addition, they almost always have emotional attitudes toward the property rooted in the memories (good or bad) associated with their time in the house or apartment. Some owners even feel that their home somehow reflects their character and take rejection by buyers personally.

A home that doesn't sell is very different from a listing that doesn't sell, even if they are one and the same property. Home sellers keep asking, "Why isn't it selling?" When answering that question and counseling a home seller, the agent must walk a narrow path through emotionally mined territory. Think about it. Should you make suggestions on home improvements that might increase the salability? Should you counsel patience, especially in a slow market? Should you give the seller an account of all the sales efforts that are being made? Should you report back on the opinions expressed by prospective buyers who looked at the house but did not make an offer? Should you suggest a price reduction?

When not wearing any of these many hats, the residential specialist attends office meetings, goes on office caravans to inspect new listings, previews properties that he or she intends to show, and usually gets in a few training and education sessions each year. And in an unofficial capacity (while still promoting career goals), he or she also attends PTA meetings, and Scouts, and Little League, and plays golf, and has lunch.

## The Money

"I'm making damn good money," says David Echols, a New Jersey real estate agent.

> But it sure is nice to have Jeanne working too. Every month, we know that the check from AT&T will be there, and we try to budget the necessities within her income. I'm also listed as a spouse on her medical and dental benefits, so that saves us money too.
>
> But don't get me wrong, we're hooked into the roller-coaster economy just like every other real estate agent. In the middle of the mid-1980s boom, we bought a second home at the shore and a boat. Then, because making the payments was virtually impossible on my 90s recession income, we sold both in 1992 (at a small profit for the shore house and a moderate loss for the boat).
>
> Does it hurt? Sure it hurts. I'm working the same hours, maybe more, and making less than half the money. But I'm sticking it out. This is a good job, and I really believe things will turn again. They've got to! All these people have to live somewhere!

The most recent survey, conducted in 1990 by the National Association of Realtors, puts the median annual income for a full-time salesperson at $22,500, with an average workweek of 42 hours. Not much for a full-time job requiring all those hats we just talked about! But remember, many agents are making more.

Of those who are making less, many list themselves as full-time because they don't have another job, but in reality they work less than a 40-hour week.

In his book, *Your Successful Real Estate Career*, Kenneth Edwards reminds readers of the common real estate saw, "Ten percent of the agents do 90 percent of the business." That same 10 percent also take home 90 percent of the salesperson's share of residential real estate commissions in the United States.

Which brings us to splits. As a licensed salesperson, you must work under the supervision of a licensed broker. Some licensed brokers may also choose to work as salespeople in an agency owned by another broker or group of brokers. Most agents who work in the role of salesperson split the commissions they earn with the agency in which they work. The most common commission split is 50/50, with incentives. The incentives are usually better ratios for those who bring in more business. For example, after the first $25,000 in earned commissions, the split may change to 60/40 in the salesperson's favor. It may even change to 70/30 for top earners.

Some licensed salespeople and brokers get 100 percent of earned commissions, even though they work under the supervision of another broker. These agents have contractual arrangements with their broker in which they agree to "rent" their desk space, pay their own telephone bills, and pay all the expenses of marketing the properties they list.

For residential salespeople, there are no salaries, no hourly wages. Everything the salesperson takes home is earned through commissions on property that has been sold. However, "sold" has two sides. A salesperson will get a portion of the commission on every listing that he or she brings in if and when the property sells during the term of the listing, even if another agent actually does the selling. On the other hand, a part of the commission on every property a salesperson sells is also paid over to the listing agency and the listing salesperson. So there's a lot of dividing, and by the time all the dividing is done, a salesperson's share of the $18,000 commission check on a $300,000 sale will probably be about $4,500.

But take note: Selling or holding the listing on six properties sold at $300,000 each, all with 6 percent commissions, will *not* bring in a net income of $27,000. As independent contractors working for brokers, salespeople must absorb a lot of expenses.

Cars are the worst. You must have a good one because you will be driving your customers from listing to listing in it. You must also pay for gas, repairs, and insurance out of your own pocket, although these expenses are tax-deductible if documented for business use.

Beyond the expenses for your car, you will also have to pay self-employment tax, which is approximately double the social security deduction you'd pay if employed in a salaried job. You'll pay your own health care insurance and establish your own retirement fund. There are no paid vacations and few company lunches or paid business trips. Some brokers even insist that salespeople share some of the listing expenses.

The good news is that you won't have to wait for a promotion to reap financial rewards for outstanding work. You'll be paid for your success at every closing. Also, since housing usually keeps pace with inflation or leads it, your income will maintain itself in real dollars.

## The People

"The people thing is a love/hate relationship for me," says Anna Peralta, a salesperson in Texas. "I really like helping buyers and sellers, and sometimes we become friends. But I hate the money part. Even the nicest people can get nasty over money. So you learn to protect yourself. You stick to the schedules you make, and you don't give up your free time at the drop of a hat. You hedge a lot."

Good and bad experiences in dealing with customers and clients are just about what everyone would expect in a service-oriented business. Many sales agents, however, feel that the real people problems in residential real estate (those nagging headaches and sometimes even heartaches) are generated by professional relationships. Nevertheless, these same agents are quick to admit that so are the moments of camaraderie and gratitude and even admiration.

"I have a lot of friends and acquaintances who are sales agents in my office and other offices," continues Peralta.

And I like being with them. But you can never be completely at ease. There's this competition thing. You have to be careful that you don't give away a lead on a listing because when it comes right down to it, your "friend" will usually try for that listing just as hard as you do. And sales are even worse. I was in a bidding war once with another agent in my own office, and it was like a *real* war, like we never knew each other, had never had lunch together. Her customers outbid mine finally, and she made the deal. We're friends again now, but not quite like before.

Janet Houde, a salesperson in California's Silicon Valley, has a different perspective. She finds negotiating the most challenging part of the job, but also the most satisfying. "Working with the numbers and the people, getting it together, making the deal—that's what really builds your self-image. And people are really grateful. They know how hard you work."

Houde's optimism and positive attitude toward people are factors in her success at another growing work style in residential sales: the salespersons' partnership. Like Houde, many agents with children at home find the odd hours and the drop-every-thing-and-run demands of the career incongruous with a "normal" family life. "You *have* to keep that appointment with the orthodontist," she says, "and you *want* to be at your child's debut in the school play." She is able to schedule more effectively and cover unexpected demands with less disruption to her life by sharing both responsibilities and income with a partner.

The two work as a team, compensating for each other's weaknesses and building on each other's strengths. They cover for each other both on short notice calls and during vacations and long weekend breaks. All income is split 50/50. This type of arrangement requires trust, honesty, and dedication from both partners. When it works, it works very well, and the whole becomes greater than the sum of its parts, to borrow from an old axiom.

Another aspect of personal interaction in the career of the residential specialist is supervision. Technically, a licensed salesperson cannot perform a single act in the role of agent without the supervision of a broker. But *supervision* has a wide play between a tight rein and a free rein. Some salespeople virtually never see their bosses, whereas others are held tight with suggestions, guidelines, meetings, evaluations, and checkpoints.

The same can be said of training. Some small, independent brokers give their salespeople excellent one-to-one training; others let them sink or swim on their own. Most agencies affiliated with one of the national franchises let the franchise train the neophyte agent. Most large multioffice agencies have in-house training programs.

When there's a training manual, however, there's usually a bureaucracy too—and a procedures manual and individual competency appraisals and titles and promotions. In real estate brokerage firms where the number of administrative personnel is almost as large as the number of agents out working with the public, the job of residential salesperson can take on the characteristics of almost any white-collar job in many American corporations.

## Getting In

All real estate agents must be licensed, and all licensing is done at the state level. Every state requires that prospective salespeople pass a standardized written licensing exam, but the requirements for eligibility to take the exam and get the license differ. To get information on the requirements in your state, contact the appropriate real estate commission listed in Appendix III.

Preparation courses for the licensing exam are often required by the state. These are given in private real estate schools, in community adult school programs, in community colleges, and in state-supported and private four-year colleges and universities.

Some real estate firms advertise for new salespeople in the help-wanted sections of local newspapers. Often these firms will offer to pay for the required schooling if a prospective agent agrees to work for the firm for a specified length of time. Some even offer to pay without a written commitment. Many larger firms also have in-house training programs that supplement the required study programs.

In this career, however, the problem is not getting in, but rather staying in. Once you have a license, there is a period of at least six months during which you must adapt to the new job and begin to build up your client and customer base. (A client is a person who lists with you; a customer is a prospective buyer.)

Throughout that entire six months, you may not have any income! Even if you are fortunate enough to sell a property in the first three months of your employment, it probably won't close for at least an additional six weeks. Because you won't collect any commission until your sale or listing closes, all of that time is work-time without pay.

These agents who plan for this getting-started period are more likely to survive and succeed than those who are anxious for an immediate sale and immediate income. Some new agents hold onto moonlighting jobs until they get their real estate careers established. Others have a spouse who provides the steady (pay-the-rent) income while the real estate–generated income is used to provide "the good life."

For those agents who survive their novice period and plan to continue as residential specialists, a subgroup of the National Association of Realtors (the Residential Sales Council of the Realtors National Marketing Institute) awards a Certified Residential Specialist (CRS) designation. The designation requires the completion of formal study programs and the demonstration of competence. For more information, contact the designation co-ordinator of the Member Services Department at (800) 462-8841, extension 4448.

### Is This for You?

How do you feel about telephone calls at 11 P.M.—calls in which a customer asks, "What color is the kitchen in the house on Maple Street?" They happen, and you've got to handle them if you are to survive as a real estate salesperson.

Doing so in a way that allows you to remain sane requires both self-confidence and resolve, two aspects of the positive self-image that is the most important factor in achieving success in this career. The person who thinks well of him- or herself will not allow the job to become overwhelming. Personal time will be protected. Professional standing will be maintained. As an agent with a positive self-image, you will be able to tell the late-night caller that you do not accept business calls after 9 P.M. And you will *not* answer the caller's question until the next morning!

"Residential sales can eat you up!" says Janet Houde. "I've survived and prospered because I've kept the job in perspective. The agent who keeps a steady pace survives; the flash in the pan has often gone on to another career before the third year. Part of keeping a steady pace is consistency. The best agents don't blow hot and cold. Their performance is consistent; it can be counted on. And, of course, honesty and fairness go without saying."

In addition to strong character, residential real estate sales also requires flexibility. Are you willing to work on a different schedule every day? Are you willing to work evenings? Weekends? Can you accept customers who suddenly change their minds after you have spent weeks showing a selected area or housing style? Can you adapt your work to the needs of a large variety of customers and clients? Can you be price-conscious with one buyer and status-conscious with another?

Finally, are you willing to farm? To be successful in this business, you've got to knock on doors, write letters, and make phone calls to total strangers. You've got to be a part of the community, a volunteer and a joiner, and you've got to let everyone you meet know that you work in real estate.

Residential real estate sales is a career of many tasks and many skills, but one requirement is common to all of them: You've got to like, really like, people. It can almost be said that the residential real estate salesperson is not in a sales career at all. He or she is in a helping career, a profession with a fiduciary role. Unless you are willing to maintain and deserve the trust of the people you serve, you will find the job excruciatingly demanding, and you will not survive. On the other hand, if you serve the public well, you will enjoy the benefits of referrals based on your reputation. The work of this career will become easier and easier, and the rewards greater and greater.

## For More Information

The National Association of Realtors has a free booklet titled *Careers in Real Estate*. Request form 116-30 when you write to the NAR at the address given in Appendix I.

Local Realtor Boards have material available on licensing requirements and career opportunities. Call or stop in.

An excellent guide to the day-to-day problems and situations of the job is *Your Successful Real Estate Career*, by Kenneth W. Edwards (New York: AMACOM, 1987), $10.95. Write to the American Management Association, 135 W. 50th St., New York, NY 10020.

# Who's Minding the Store?

## *The Broker/Office Manager*

Every single real estate office in the country—not every real estate *company*, mind you, but every single *office* (even if it's one room with a sign on the door)—must have a licensed broker of record. That broker might be the owner of the firm or a broker/ office manager who reports to the man, woman, or corporation whose name appears on the sign. In either case, he or she is responsible.

Responsible for what? For just about everything. In the business of being the agent in the sale of real estate, every written offer is presented to the seller under the name of a broker, even if a salesperson does all the selling and all the presenting. In the business of listing real estate, a salesperson may take a listing, but there's no legal agency relationship until the broker of record signs the listing contract and returns it to the seller. In every state in the United States, only licensed real estate brokers can enter into contracts to act as agents in the buying and selling of real property.

"Whoa!" you cry. "What about that chapter I just read about residential sales agents. Sounds to me like they act as agents!"

They do. But only as representatives of the broker under whose guidance they work. Theoretically, the salesperson can do nothing without the knowledge and permission of his or her broker, and the broker is responsible for everything the salesperson does. So read on. Here, in the career of broker, lies the better part of both the power and the responsibility in many aspects of the real estate marketplace.

## The Work

Although there is often some overlap, most men and women who hold a broker's license work in one of three capacities: the selling broker, the office manager, or the administrative broker. We'll introduce you to the work of the administrative broker in Chapter 19, "In the Real Estate Corporation," but you'll have to read several chapters to explore thoroughly the career possibilities of the selling broker.

You might, for example, find a selling broker working in residential real estate listing and sales. Or you might come across selling brokers who specialize in commercial leasing or land development sales. Some brokers are rental specialists, and some work in relocation. In all these instances, the selling broker chooses to work "in the field" which means with the clients and the properties. His or her routines and responsibilities correspond exactly to the work of the licensed salesperson in that specialty.

For those real estate agents who do not want to remain in sales, a broker's license is often the doorway to a management career. Like careers in most other types of business administration, it has two paths: owning your own company or working as the manager of a branch office in a large multioffice firm. The day-to-day work on both paths, however, is basically the same. It falls into three general categories: recruiting and training, supervising, and planning and leadership.

*Recruiting and training* new salespeople is an ongoing and time-consuming responsibility that is essential to the life of the business. Ronald Buford, owner of Buford Realty in Conroe, Texas, explains that it's very difficult now to get new agents and, more important, to keep them. He estimates that the average career of a new real estate agent is about 18 months.

"People enter the field for the wrong reasons," he speculates. "They don't know what they're getting into, and when the work is not what they expected, they leave."

To avoid taking on new agents who will leave before they even begin to succeed, Buford interviews every candidate personally. When he does welcome a new agent on board, he carefully oversees what he calls "field training" by accompanying the agent through several months of showings, negotiations, and listings.

Even in larger offices where new agents are assigned to experienced agents in mentor programs, the office manager is still called on for both training and counseling. In franchises and multioffice firms where there are formal training programs, it's the office manager who is expected to help the new recruit turn the theory into practice. And once new agents are on their own, the office manager must be available to answer the inevitable questions that come up in virtually every deal.

Because the broker is legally responsible for the professional actions of all salespeople affiliated with the office, *supervision* also takes up a large part of each day. In the real estate business, however, the word *supervision* has a somewhat different connotation than in other businesses, where it refers to the close watching of employees who perform agreed-on tasks and are paid a set wage. The reasons for this difference are the demands of the job, earnings by commission, and the need for a license.

Generally, aspiring real estate agents are responsible and ambitious people to begin with. When they enter the career, they already know that they won't succeed (and therefore won't get paid) if they don't keep appointments, meet commitments, and come to work on time. They also know that they'll lose their licenses if they lie or cheat or steal.

So the supervision part of a broker's job is not as much watching as it is advising. The broker is careful to steer and guide agents who wander into any of real estate law's gray areas, such as buyer representation or seller knowledge of undisclosed faults in a house. The broker often advises on the techniques of doing a competitive market analysis, on reductions of asking price and extensions of the listing contract, on negotiating strategies, and on financing opportunities. And finally, it is the broker who writes the checks that pay the salespeople their share of commissions.

Going a step further, there's the "higher" meaning of the word *supervision*. Because real estate is a service rather than a task-oriented job, success often depends on one's ability to self-start and keep going. Supervising, therefore, can also mean motivating, which for many top owners and managers is the sine qua non of their jobs.

Patricia Lawless is among them. As the broker/office manager of the Long & Foster office in Centreville, Virginia, she strives for excellence in the performance of Realtor services and self-fulfillment and satisfaction among the salespeople in her office. She names motivation and support as the most important parts of her job.

"Sometimes," she comments, "I feel almost like a cheerleader!"

The *planning and leadership* aspect of the broker/office manager's work involves finding ways to focus that cheerleading to increase the income of each salesperson and therefore the profitability of the office. Lawless sees planning as the key to achieving that focus. "In my office, I set up a structure within which the salesperson can succeed," she says. She helps each of her agents set his or her own goals, and then she schedules weekly meetings to evaluate the progress toward those goals.

Besides the management of people, the broker/office manager must also manage the logistics of the business. The advertising must be designed and scheduled, the office equipment purchased and maintained, floor time scheduled, support personnel hired and supervised, stationery and supplies ordered, bills paid, and the profit/loss position monitored monthly. In large multioffice firms, the office manager must also save some time for meetings with upper management.

Because of the unstructured day that is characteristic of all real estate sales work, another important aspect of the broker/ office manager's job is time management: his or her own time, the time of the support staff, and, to some extent, the time of the salespeople. When managing salespeople, however, many brokers find the line between too much time structure and too much freedom a difficult one to walk.

## The Money

According to their nationwide survey, the National Association of Realtors reports that the median gross personal income for a broker/owner in 1990 (after expenses) was $31,000, down 12 percent from the 1988 high of $35,000. This income survey was not conducted in 1992, but NAR projections indicate that there was little change. 1994 results will be available from NAR headquarters in Chicago in 1995. The actual income of individual brokers varies greatly, however, depending on the area of the country and the size of the firm. Many top performers get into the six-figure range.

These numbers tell only a small part of the financial story, however. It's in the way earnings are determined that some of the major differences between the careers of the broker/owner and the broker/office manager become apparent. Most office managers are guaranteed by contract to receive a monthly salary, plus an agreed-on percentage of their office's profits (usually paid as a bonus at the end of the fiscal year). Many broker/owners also budget a monthly salary for themselves, but there are no guarantees that they'll get it unless the firm's income is adequate. In the final analysis, each broker/owner's annual income depends completely on the profitability of the firm.

Perhaps an even more basic difference between the careers of broker/owner and broker/office manager is the amount of capital that the individual must put up to establish an office in the first place. Here we run into the age-old question of whether it's better to own your own small business or be a part of a large company. The small business offers its owner unlimited possibility but high risk. The large company offers its employee support and security but limited autonomy. One demands money; the other doesn't.

Pat Lawless had worked as a salesperson for Long & Foster for six years when she recognized the potential for a branch office in Centreville. She made a recommendation to the corporate offices and waited. It took two years before she got the go-ahead. Then she found a location and opened an office with eight salespeople. Today, she's managing 90 agents out of that same office. The total cost of this business venture to her was $0.

"The major advantage in going with an established large firm is that you use the firm's capitalization," she says. Other office managers also mention bulk-purchase discounts as an added advantage because the firm saves significantly on office supplies, equipment, and advertising costs. And virtually everyone in the business agrees with Lawless when she says, "It's easier to build a business when you have the image equity of a firm with a well-known name."

For those who want to be sole owner as well as manager, Ronald Buford estimates that "you need $125,000 to $150,000 to open an independent office that will survive in today's economy. In addition, you'll need between two to four years before the business really begins to earn you a living. People who try to open an independent office on a shoestring usually fail. If you can't afford to put in the money to establish your name, the franchise route is more efficient for a new beginning."

There are more than a dozen major real estate franchises operating in the United States. You can probably name several off the top of your head: Century 21, The Prudential, RE/MAX,

Coldwell Banker, ERA, and Realty World to start. Each charges a franchise fee for buying into the organization. The franchise fee plus start-up costs for a new office usually run between $50,000 and $100,000.

Every franchise office owner also pays certain fees each year. Jerry Sowards, co-owner of Century 21 Sowards Realtors in Memphis, Tennessee, reports paying a token annual fee, plus 6 percent of every dollar as a service fee for support and advice and 2 percent of every dollar for national advertising. He also buys all his stationery and office supplies through the Century 21 office.

Is it worth it? Sowards thinks so. "We wanted a small office with a big name," he says. "The Century 21 name allows us to compete with those brokers who have seven or eight hundred people working for them."

## The People

For fairness and efficiency, written policies and procedures are usually established whenever *management* means managing people. Every broker/owner must set up procedures by which to run the business in order to keep the sales staff working as a team and to maintain the image of the company. Every broker/office manager must set up the day-to-day procedures of the office within the policies and procedures guidelines of the main office. When a franchise is involved, the headquarters and regional offices also dictate certain policies. The quality and effectiveness of the written policies and procedures often determine how people interact with one another within the company.

Perhaps the best example is a success story. In less than 25 years, Weichert Realtors has grown from a one-office firm in Chatham, New Jersey, to one of the largest independent firms in the nation. Jim Weichert attributes much of that success to teamwork, and the teamwork seems to thrive within structure.

Denise Smith, the firm's public relations representative, points out that all the policies and procedures that make the corporation a continuing success were in place when Jim Weichert was running a one-man office. They are built around a few simple directives: Pay attention to the customer! Do it now! Follow through! Communicate!

In most successful offices, communication between the broker and the sales force is a top priority. Whether the firm has a staff of four, 40, 400, or 4,000, the role of broker requires both a healthy respect for the individual salesperson and a healthy regard for efficiency and structure. Policies and procedures manuals should support these goals and foster communication, self-esteem, and efficiency. However, that's too big an assignment for words and paper, so we come back to the people. The broker's attitudes and actions always make a tremendous difference in the working atmosphere of an office and in its ultimate success.

But that's not all. Virtually every broker in the nation will tell you that real estate is a service business. As a manager in this business, the broker must also be aware of and attend to the needs of buyers, sellers, and the community.

Some brokers, like Beverly Sikorski, enjoy the contact with the public so much that they never give it up. Owner and manager of RE/MAX of Ann Arbor, Michigan, Sikorski spends about 50 percent of her time on management and 50 percent on sales. "Working with people is the best part of the job!" she declares.

Ronald Buford has the same attitude. "Real estate is a personal business," he says, "and my greatest pleasure is the personal aspect. The husband/father and wife/mother who are looking for a house are different from the same people as a man and woman in the workplace. And the children are extremely important. I always pay attention to the children. I enjoy building relationships with people, and real estate sales gives me that opportunity."

## Getting In

Every state requires that you pass a licensing examination before you can become a real estate broker. In most states, you must also do specialized course work, with the requirements ranging from a minimum number of hours at a real estate school to completion of several college-level programs of study. In some states, ongoing professional education is a requirement for license renewal.

Most states also require that all applicants have one or more years of experience in the business, usually as a licensed salesperson. And all states require evidence of good character and a "clean record" which means no convictions for felonies of any kind.

Regarding credentials, as of this writing, those who can pass the licensing exam do not need a college degree of any kind to be a broker. But that exam is *not* easy, and anyone who can pass it probably could hold a degree. Licensing requirements for your state are available from the state real estate commission. Addresses and telephone numbers are listed in Appendix III.

Getting established as a broker/office manager, however, goes beyond getting a license. If you choose to open your own business, you must be willing to take a sizable financial risk. In addition, you'll most likely want to join the National Association of Realtors (the largest trade organization in the country), your local Multiple Listing Service, and the local, state, and national specialty groups within the NAR that apply to the business of your office. Joining these groups will, of course, involve dues and fees and a required commitment to the group's code of ethics.

Those who aspire to manage an office in a large multioffice firm usually get in through the "show-me" method. That is, they establish outstanding performance records. Often they join the firm with a salesperson's license, sell houses or commercial property for the required period of time, get their broker's license, and then work as a selling broker/associate. At that point, some of them, like Pat Lawless, convince the upper management that a new office should be opened. Others wait for a vacancy in one of the established offices.

This kind of advancement into office management is not without problems, however. Sometimes, the best salespeople are not the best office managers. Some brokers try office management and then return to sales. For others, office management leads to specialized management roles within the real estate corporation, roles such as sales manager, general manager, training manager, or perhaps the management of a corporation division, such as relocation, commercial leasing, residential rentals, asset management, or mortgage brokerage.

For those with experience and a commitment to a career in brokerage management, the Real Estate Brokerage Managers Council of the NAR offers a Certified Real Estate Brokerage Manager (CRB) designation. The CRB is awarded after successful completion of certain education and experience requirements, which are set forth in the rules and regulations of the organization. For information on these requirements, call the Council's Membership Department at (312) 321-4435.

## Is This for You?

Like Janus, the Roman god who looked two ways, the broker/ office manager must attend equally to two career concerns. He or she must know and practice both the business of real estate and the techniques of good management.

Knowing the business of real estate means knowing real estate law, real estate valuation, real estate finance, and real estate negotiation. It means knowing how to get a listing and sell a property. It means knowing advertising and marketing techniques. And it means keeping abreast of all the current local, regional, and national events, issues, and trends that relate to the business.

Practicing the techniques of good management means motivating and supervising the staff, working for effective communication, and controlling costs. It means planning and evaluating. Sometimes it means taking risks, and always it is demanding. Whether as the authority figure or the support person, the manager must be present in the office or be readily available if the business of a real estate firm is to succeed.

Are you willing to take on this load? It's not easy, and there are no guarantees. A good income, the opportunity to build and expand a business, and a high profile in the community are all carrots that might keep the going. If you choose to be an office manager in a large firm, the voices and memos of upper management might be the sticks that also encourage you to go forward. For the broker/owner, these bills that must be paid are pretty sharp-pointed stimuli too.

What kind of person does it take? One with most of the usual business skills: the ability to organize, to manage one's own time and schedule the time of others, to make decisions, to pay careful attention to details, to evaluate all aspects of a controversial situation, and to see a problem from several perspectives.

But again, that's not all. This career requires the ability to laugh, to trust while protecting one's own interests, to work with others in a team effort, and to persuade.

Plus one other quality that is often unrecognized. The successful broker needs good boundaries. Allowed free rein, the demands of this career can grow into an incessantly needy monster that allows you no recreational activities and little time for family and friends. By establishing firm boundaries between business and personal roles, the broker can be a success in this career and a normal, yes, even happy, person too!

## For More Information

Most local Realtor Boards have libraries that focus on professional and local real estate concerns. If you hold a salesperson's license, you can usually use these facilities.

Many colleges and universities offer courses and degrees in real estate. See Appendix II, "Where to Study Real Estate."

The Real Estate Brokerage Managers Council publishes *Issues and Trends*, a quarterly newsletter covering current concerns. Single copies are $6.50 for nonmembers and can be ordered from the Council. See Appendix I for address.

For an excellent overview of the business of running a real estate office, read *Real Estate Office Management: People, Functions, Systems*, 2d ed. (Chicago: Real Estate Brokerage Council, 1988), $18.95. To purchase, contact the Realtors National Marketing Institute, 430 N. Michigan Ave., Chicago, IL 60611-4092.

# CHAPTER 5

# Sold! The Career of Auctioneer

There have almost always been real estate auctions, of course, but not a noticeable number of them, and auction advertising in nontrade publications was not common. Estate sales were held occasionally. Here and there sizable residential and commercial properties went on the block after their owners ran into financial problems or felt that the attraction of an auction would sell their building or complex—and sell it fast.

But things have changed. If you get the feeling that over the last few years real estate auctions have been conducted everywhere, and pretty often too, you're right. According to the Gwent Group, a management consulting firm based in Bloomington, Indiana, the value of real property sold at auction went from $10 billion in 1980 to an estimated (at this writing) $38 billion for 1992. In a 1992 survey of 131 U.S. auction firms, the National Association of Realtors found that the number of properties offered through auctions more than doubled during the second quarter of 1991 from the first quarter of 1990, increasing to just over 81,500.

There are several reasons for today's explosion of auction activity. The sluggish real estate market of the last few years has made many owners turn to auctions to draw attention to their properties in a sea of "For Sale" signs and to rid themselves of holdings "in distress."

An important example of the latter is the Resolution Trust Corporation (RTC). Many government agencies have sold—and continue to sell—real estate at auction, but the RTC is a newcomer to this scene. Set up in 1989, it is the government-backed entity that is disposing of properties acquired from failed thrift associations in the late 1980s and early 1990s. Those problem savings and loan institutions (S&Ls) left portfolios of bad loans

Although the agency has been aggressively selling real estate for several years now, it still has billions of dollars of holdings all over the United States. The majority of properties held by the RTC are sold at auction. The agency engages the services of local auctioneers to conduct blocks of sales, sometimes several times a year in some cities and towns.

These activities, private and government-sponsored, have brought auctions from the classified sections of newspapers, sometimes only trade journals at that, to large display advertisements in the real estate sections and even main news sections of such publications as the *New York Times*. Auctions are, well, respectable now. Single-family homes, blocks of unsold condominiums, half-empty strip malls—virtually every kind of residential and commercial property has found its way to the auction block over the last few years in far greater numbers than ever before. The newfound popularity of and publicity about auctions has also meant that sellers who had never before considered the concept are now signing up to have their properties sold by the gavel.

Today, auctioneering is a serious and complex business. Although Dan the Country Auction Man still conducts small sales in rural America, he has been joined by companies like Kennedy-Wilson, Inc., the largest auction house in the industry, which has 12 offices around the world, including branches in England and Australia, and more than 300 employees worldwide. (Even the largest auction houses do not have the huge number of employees that large companies in most other fields do.) Kennedy-Wilson's 1992 auction volume was $866 million.

The National Auctioneers Association (NAA), the professional organization for this career, estimates the number of auctioneers, selling all varieties of goods, at more than 40,000. Because not every state requires licensing, exact figures are difficult to come by. There are 25,000 licensed auctioneers. About 5,400 auctioneers are members of the NAA. The NAA notes that about 1,500 auctioneers specialize in real estate auctions.

Auctioneering is, as you might expect, a very old method of selling goods. Although today's sales might be a combination of show biz and high tech, the basic concept and the running of an auction remain as simple as they were in early recorded history.

The NAA has traced the history of these sales. Do you know how far back they go?

| | |
|---|---|
| 500 B.C. | The earliest written account of auctions: Greek historian Herodotus documents Babylonian wedding auctions. (No notes on whether it was the bride being auctioned!) The word *auction* is from the Latin *auctus*, meaning "to increase." |
| Circa 10–100 A.D. | The Roman Empire is sold at auction. However, the successful bidder is soon overthrown and beheaded. |
| 1400s | Henry VII of England requires licenses for auctioneers. |
| 1712 | A Frenchman starts the tradition of auction houses when he opens an establishment that sells dissimilar goods at auction. (Sotheby's was founded in 1744, and Christie's in 1766.) |
| 1860s | The reputation of auctioneers is tarnished by sales of the spoils of the Civil War. |
| Post-1860s | A popular term for auctioneers, the honorary title of Colonel, is established after the Civil War when the U.S. Army sells its surplus goods and arms at auction and the task is assigned to colonels. Though still used occasionally, the term is not common today. |
| 1930s | The growth of auctions is inhibited by traumas experienced by families whose homes were foreclosed during the Great Depression. |
| 1991 | Real estate sold at auction tops $32 billion in the United States. Auctions are used extensively to market real estate in Europe and North America and are the prime method of marketing real estate in Australia. |

Perhaps you can easily see yourself wielding a gavel, eyes quickly scanning a crowded room, continuing the nonstop auction chant until . . . sold! Feel the adrenaline pumping? Read on.

## The Work

Realty auctioneers can sell houses, land, residential or commercial properties, shopping centers—anything that falls under the huge real estate umbrella.

Many auctioneers are self-employed, running their own companies, and others conduct sales for auction houses on a freelance basis. There is also work in the industry for those who do not go near an auction room. More about them later.

There are a half dozen or so variations on the basic auction. Some auctions require a minimum bid; others do not. Some auctions call for sealed bids. Interested buyers submit their bids by mail or fax, and the highest bid wins the property. Auctions can be silent, with bidders merely nodding or gesturing to indicate an offer. Bidders might also raise their hands, hold up cards or paddles, or use any other style of making an offer that auctioneers prefer.

Entrepreneurial auctioneers have their hands full. Specifically, they have five primary tasks.

### Find the Business

In larger houses, this task is handled by sales associates, overseen by the auctioneer, whose sole job is to bring in listings of properties for sale. Auctioneers also find the business through time-honored networking, attending the many luncheons and dinners in their home community, and traveling to local, regional, or even national areas where listings might result from contacts. Listings are vital to a successful auction company because if there are no listings, there are no sales, and auctioneers who own their own companies make money through turnover.

Finding the business also means talking to sellers, looking carefully at the properties for sale, and offering advice to clients. One point an auctioneer will raise, for instance, is the kind of auction the seller wants or the auctioneer thinks will work best, given that individual's circumstances.

### Research the Property

The next task is to research the property to arrive at a selling price acceptable to the seller. "You have to check titles, walk the property, and talk to neighbors," says Martin E. Higgenbotham of Higgenbotham Auctioneers, International, Inc., in Lakeland, Florida. "It's a complicated business." For some, assessing a property is the most difficult part of the job and is learned only through much study and experience.

Hellen B. King, one of the growing number of women in auctioneering, notes that "some people have a real talent for appraising." Can the auctioneer call in an appraiser? "We tend to look at a property with an eye toward what it will bring at auction," says King, who is part owner of a small southern auction company that conducts sales throughout her state. "Auctioneers and appraisers have different guidelines."

Auctioneers or those they designate must also learn such details of the property to be sold as boundary lines, improvements that have been made, costs for utilities, lot size, amount still owed on a mortgage, interest rate, and charges against the property, if any. They must be skilled in taxes, zoning laws, and terms of financing.

### Promote the Auction

In larger houses, promotion is handled by the public relations or advertising department. In small operations, the auctioneers do it themselves. Promotion can include newspaper ads announcing sales, radio and television spots, and brochures describing the property to be sold. Auction companies usually produce tons of printed material describing their services, announcing upcoming sales, and detailing the properties headed for the auction block.

### Plan the Sale

This task means arranging for interested buyers to view the property a week or so before the sale. Decisions must also be made about the site of the auction (will it be held at the property to be sold or at another locale, such as a hotel ballroom?), the hours of the sale, how many part-timers will be needed and for what aspect of the sale, and whether to offer financing to buyers if the sale will be fairly large (for example, will the auctioneer invite a mortgage broker company to set up a table near the auction room to provide financing assistance to buyers?).

An auction is usually scheduled three to four weeks after the auctioneer and seller agree on the sale. Indeed, every stage of these sales is fast-forwarded, with keys handed to new owners far more quickly than in conventional realty turnovers.

Commissions paid by the seller can vary, but hover around 6 percent, less for sales of multimillion-dollar properties. Sellers usually also absorb auction marketing expenses, such as hiring a space for the auction to be held, if that is necessary. The auctioneer offers expertise and staff.

"The key here is volume," notes Higgenbotham, who is also a past president of the NAA. "When you take a listing in a traditional real estate agency," he continues, "you can assume that fewer than 50 percent of those properties will sell through that office. In the auction business, you know that 100 percent of the properties you list will sell."

### Conduct the Sale

Some auction house owners do not get out on the floor and actually conduct the sale but have employees for that purpose; some are not even on the premises on auction day. But those who *are* may do the auction calling or perhaps just mingle among the crowd taking a nose count, chatting with bidders, and keeping an eye on employees. What they certainly are doing is not missing a trick.

The show business aspect of auctions was mentioned earlier. More than one of these sales has featured local high school cheerleaders parading onto the auction floor, complete with pom-poms. Auction company owners must be creative in getting—and keeping—the auction crowd "pumped up" to make a sale successful.

"Hmmm," you say. "That's fine about the auctioneer who owns his own company, but aren't there other positions in auction houses?"

Joseph G. Keefhaver, executive director of the NAA, notes that the term *auctioneer* can be used by those who never wield a gavel. It is certainly used by many who do not own auction companies. Let's look inside the larger houses.

The largest income can be made by the sales associates who bring in the business. Higgenbotham's firm has a sales staff of 30 full-time workers around the country. This is commissions-only work, and sales associates' paychecks are based on volume. In many instances, a sales associate need only bring in a listing, then he or she is free to go after the next one. Once a for-sale property is in-house, it travels through the appropriate departments until the day of the auction. Some companies ask that a sales associate attend the auction for his or her listing; others do not. At some companies, associates maintain a liaison with sellers throughout the auction process. Take this minimal involvement, add the high number of sales that an auction house must produce to stay profitable, and the commissions stack up impressively.

Another opportunity in an auction company is for those known as ring associate, bid assistants, or bid consultants. These are the men and women who "work the crowd" on auction day, answering bidders' questions. Ring associates must be *very* fast: quick on their feet and adept at using a hand-held calculator. They answer all types of questions from those in the auction audience, mostly about financing. Good ring people are vital to an auctioneer. Not only must they be able to help people make decisions during the fast-moving auction process, they must also keep some would-be buyers from making wrong decisions. If someone in the audience is bidding beyond his potential for financing or affording the property, a good ring associate will "shut him down," that is, tell him that his income stream will not allow him to make payments on the property that interests him. Ring people need to be experienced and are often one-time auctioneers.

There is a lot of movement in this field; very little is cast in stone regarding staff. For example, a busy auction house might employ a few auctioneers, who actually call the sales, on a per diem or per-sale basis. Kennedy-Wilson operates in this manner. Auctioneers, like ring people, must of course travel to where the auctions are for the company that engages them.

In another vein, a large nationwide company moving into Midtown USA for a sale might engage the services of an auction company in Midtown either to supplement its own staff or to add strength in a particular area of the auction process.

King is a good example of the varied work to be done in an auction house. Her background includes an MBA earned in the late 1970s, work for the Social Security Administration, and real estate sales, both residential and commercial. She joined a conventional real estate office to develop a nonauction program for the company, which was on the brink of deciding to handle auctions exclusively. Now she is half owner of the company, which has five permanent employees and another ten engaged on a per diem basis.

She holds the title chief financial officer and vice-president. Her principal work is putting together marketing proposals. She attends most of her company's scheduled auctions and does some auctioneering herself. She recalls, "It was scary at first, but I learned you can't be self-conscious. Just get out there and do the job and forget yourself."

## The Money

It is difficult to gauge the income of auctioneers who own their own companies. "It's all over the field," says Keefhaver of the NAA. Indeed, because this is such an entrepreneurial field, incomes can vary widely. One rather old survey might be of help in determining remuneration. Some 321 participants in a 1988 and 1989 Certified Auctioneers Institute (CAI) survey, comprising those taking courses leading to certification as well as those who had signed up for advanced courses, were asked about a number of different issues in the business, including income. When it came to personal annual gross income from auctions, here were the responses from the 97 percent of the participants who answered this question:

| | |
|---|---|
| under $35,000 | 36.7% |
| $35,000–$49,000 | 23.5% |
| $50,000–$99,000 | 23.4% |
| $100,000–$149,999 | 9.3% |
| $150,000–$199,999 | 3.2% |
| $200,000 and above | 3.9% |

Sales associates' incomes, based on commissions, follow the pattern of conventional real estate agents' earnings. The producers make the money. In this field, however, because there is such a rapid turnover in properties, you can take the top earner for a conventional agency and multiply his or her income a few times to estimate the income for a sales associate.

Ring people are paid by the day or by the project. Per diem fees usually run $50 to $100. Some ring people who work for houses that conduct many sales can supplement auction-day work with research on properties to be sold, for which they are paid on a per-project basis.

## The People

As mentioned earlier, the professional association for auctioneers is the National Auctioneers Association, which is based in Overland Park, Kansas.

A little less than one-half of all states require licensing of auctioneers. Some also require auctioneers, ring people, and sales associates to hold real estate licenses. In states with no licensing requirement, anyone can call him- or herself an auctioneer and hang out a shingle. On the local level, most municipalities call for a license to conduct an auction. This is actually more like a permit. You can call your state department of professional regulations to see if licensing of auctioneers is required in your area, or you can contact the Certified Auctioneers Institute.

The CAI, which is affiliated with the NAA, offers courses, in conjunction with Indiana University, leading to the CAI professional designation. Applicants for the designation must have been employed full time in the auction business for at least two years. Previous attendance at auction school is not mandatory, but most CAI applicants have attended.

In light of the recent popularity of real estate auctions, the CAI now offers a special series of informational courses, the Accredited Auctioneer of Real Estate (AARE) program. These four courses lead to the AARE professional designation and are offered periodically in cities around the United States.

## Getting In

First, the serious student should attend virtually every auction he or she can, whether it's real estate, cattle, unclaimed or seized government property, or automobiles. It is important to become familiar with the tempo, the chant, the items sold, the opening bid—the whole auction milieu.

Next comes auction school. More than 20 schools around the United States offer concentrated one-, two-, or three-week courses teaching bid calling, selling a client on an auction, preparing advertising, and other finely focused subjects in this area.

What happens after you graduate? That is difficult to answer in this field. Auction schools have no placement offices, and those in the field say that the dropout rate in and after school is extremely high. Why? One professional, echoing others, mentioned the hard work required and the difficulty entering the field. He added, though, that "the ones who want it the most make it, just like anywhere else in life."

Established auction companies are leery of offering beginners entry-level jobs for the usual reason. In this entrepreneurial field, owners figure, you train a novice and he or she leaves in two years and sets up shop just down the road from you. If you want to be an auctioneer or gain auction experience and not work in an auction house in another capacity, you'll have to be creative, perhaps while you are still applying to houses that interest you.

Higgenbotham faced the how-do-I-get-started problem when he entered the business some 30 years ago. After attending auction school in his early 20s, he returned to his hometown with no job and no prospects. What he did next shows why he is now owner of a successful, 52-person auction company.

Higgenbotham walked up and down the streets and thought. "There was an elderly lady I knew from my childhood," he recalled, "and she was going to sell the contents of her home. That's how I made my first sale. I conducted the sale for her. The gross was $350 and I worked for a 5 percent commission, so you can see how little I made. Then I went on to a bigger sale and earned $700. I collected a lot of $400 and $500 commissions until I got credibility. But if the community sees you're gutsy enough to keep going, and you're going to be around town for a while, you'll eventually be accepted."

He also suggests, for the truly intrepid, "You can buy your way into the business. If a guy is serious about getting into auctions, he'll buy himself $10,000 worth of antiques and sell them—at auction, of course. The same with real estate. He buys a house and sells it at auction. Of course you've got to be prepared to take a loss—there are no safety nets in this business."

Auctioneering used to be pretty much an occupation for men only. That has changed, and although all things are not equal here just as they are not in many other fields, women *have* noticed a difference. King recalls, "Acceptance is greater today. I can remember early on feeling really left out and not a part of the auction community—not by buyers or sellers, but by other auctioneers. That has changed dramatically."

## Is This for You?

Higgenbotham remembers an auction he attended when he was five years old. "I bought a pair of boots for a dime, and I was hooked." Others, like King, enter through a side door, but she too concedes, "After going to one or two, the fever sort of hit me." Whenever and however the auction bug bites, bite you it must. Unlike many other real estate careers, auctioneering seems to be almost in the blood of those who succeed and those who are setting out determined to become good.

True love of the business and the willingness to work hard are the first criteria for this field. Also needed is integrity, a trait mentioned over and over again by professionals. In auctioneering, you work for the seller, but you must also be careful not to offer misinformation to perhaps hundreds of interested buyers. "This calls for a straight shooter," says King. "It takes the ability to walk away from business when you know it's not going to do what it needs to do for your seller."

Higgenbotham notes, "I get these guys who call me and say, 'I want to learn how to talk fast.' Fine, go learn to talk fast, but don't become an auctioneer. You can always do charity auctions once in a while. Or I hear, 'When I retire, I'm going into the auction business.' There's a world of time and effort spent in this business. An auctioneer must know more than buyers and sellers put together."

There are some misconceptions about this arena. For example, you do not need a booming voice to conduct an auction. You do need a clear, firm one, however. The auction chant, as the NAA explains it, is a series of numbers with filler words thrown in to create a rhythm. An auctioneer varies the speed of the chant to accommodate the experience level of the crowd.

You do not have to have a particularly extroverted personality to become an auctioneer, although being outgoing to some degree and genuinely liking people certainly help. This is, after all, *sales*.

King brings up an interesting point: "I know that with conventional real estate agents if you don't put out a sign this week, you'll do it next week. People like those—and I have been one—find the transition to auctions particularly hard because of how deadline-oriented this specialty is."

As you have read in the preceding pages, this is self-employed, commissions-only, or per diem work unless you find your way into some other sort of position. There is not much security here, although the hard worker can certainly make a decent, sometimes very fine, living.

There seems to be plenty of auction business now, thanks to S&L properties, bank foreclosures, and other distress sales. What about a few years down the road? Will auctioneering retreat to the back-burner position it held before the late 1980s?

Sales of S&L properties may continue to the end of this decade. Also, now that auctions have become a high-profile way to dispose of properties, more sellers are likely to turn to them as a first choice.

Speaking optimistically about the future of the field, Higgenbotham says, "We've handled only one RTC auction in our life. Fewer than 10 percent of my sales ever have had anything to do with the RTC or bank foreclosures. We've never chased bankruptcy courts. There *is* opportunity for the right person."

King adds, "The better the economy, the better the choice of an auction because with an auction you don't have a ceiling. In good times the seller is in a better position to realize more dollars."

## For More Information

*Sold! The Professional's Guide to Real Estate Auctions*, by Stephen J. Martin and Thomas E. Battle III (Chicago: Dearborn Financial Publishing, 1991), provides general information and specific auction tactics for vacant land and residential, commercial, agricultural, and industrial properties. Sample contracts, financial tables, and checklists are included. It is available at bookstores or directly from the publisher. Write to Dearborn Financial Publishing Co., 520 N. Dearborn St., Chicago, IL 60610, or call (312) 836-4440. The price is $32.95 plus $5.00 for shipping and sales tax, where applicable.

# Selling Money

## Mortgage Bankers and Mortgage Brokers

Back in the ancient history of American home mortgage lending (the 1950s and 1960s for most of us), virtually no one had ever heard of a mortgage broker or a mortgage banker. In fact, very few existed. After all, why would anyone need one? Home financing was so simple: You saved and saved, and when you finally had the down payment, you financed your first home through your neighborhood savings bank. You could choose a "conventional" mortgage or a government-insured or government-guaranteed mortgage. That was it! Putting a second mortgage on your home was considered a flirtation with financial disaster, a serious sin, or both.

Then we had the 1980s! Single parents, blended families, and significant others entered the home buying marketplace. The S&L debacle and the ensuing bailout virtually wiped out America's neighborhood savings institutions. Huge commercial banks, credit unions, insurance companies, and other businesses entered the home mortgage marketplace. These lenders advertised ARMs, wraparounds, graduated payment plans, negative amortization, home equity lines, private mortgage insurance, bimonthly payment plans, balloons, RAMs, the APR, and a regular alphabet soup of other offerings or restrictions. Home financing grew into an intimidating process, and it became more and more difficult to strike the best possible match between a home buyer and an available mortgage plan.

That's the bad news. The good news is that career opportunities in mortgage banking and mortgage brokerage are growing exponentially *because* of the changes in the mortgage marketplace. Mortgage brokers went from a market share of near zero in 1980 to originating over 45 percent of the home mortgages written in 1991, a total of $243 billion. If you add in mortgage bankers, this service-based profession now accounts for a majority of new home mortgages each year in the United States, and that market share will most likely continue to increase.

If you're thinking, "But what exactly do they *do*?" you're not alone. Most Americans don't understand the organization of the mortgage marketplace. In fact, consumer confusion is a factor in the phenomenal increase in the number of mortgage bankers and mortgage brokers in the United States over the past five years. Beyond their roles as loan sales agents and processors, today's mortgage professionals act as counselors to home buyers.

Both mortgage bankers and mortgage brokers originate loans, which means that they find a ready, willing, and able borrower and a ready, willing, and able lender and bring them together. The vast majority of mortgage bankers and mortgage brokers also process the loans they originate. Processing includes helping the borrowers complete the application forms and keeping them informed about what to expect during the lending process, preparing the loan documents to the lender's specifications, arranging for appraisals and inspections, transmitting completed forms to the lender, and recording and documenting the loan transaction in accordance with local laws.

Most mortgage bankers are also mortgage brokers, and some mortgage brokers are also mortgage bankers. So what's the difference? Servicing. Mortgage *bankers* service the loans they originate; mortgage *brokers* do not.

Servicing includes collecting the monthly loan payments, maintaining escrow accounts for payment of taxes and insurance, and dealing with any delinquencies and other problems that may arise. The difference between banker and broker from the borrower's perspective is really point of contact.

With a loan originated by a mortgage broker, once the purchase is closed, the borrower will make payments directly to the lender, which will probably be a bank or insurance company. The home buyer has no further contact with the mortgage broker. With a loan originated by a mortgage banker, the purchase may have been financed with money provided by the mortgage banker, but the mortgage is usually sold into the secondary mortgage market soon after the closing. This means that the Federal National Mortgage Association (Fannie Mae) or an insurance company, credit union, or pension fund may actually hold the mortgage, but the borrower will continue to send payments to the originating mortgage banker. The mortgage banker remains the point of contact for the home buyer until the mortgage is paid out.

Perhaps this is beginning to sound a bit like the world of high finance to you and perhaps you're thinking, "Looks like too many numbers after the dollar sign for me." But don't count yourself out of this career yet!

You don't need a Harvard MBA, and you don't need a bank account that resembles Ross Perot's to begin a career as a mortgage banker or broker. Almost one in five mortgage brokerage firms consists of one person working out of his or her home. On the other hand, many mortgage bankers and brokers work as a part of a large corporation, with the usual health care, vacation, and retirement benefits.

## The Work

"I rarely leave my house before ten in the morning," says John Huddleton, a self-employed mortgage broker in California.

> This just isn't an early morning job. Actually, it isn't a job with regular working hours at all. I make my own schedule. A lot of it's stopping at real estate offices to keep ties intact so that I'll get referrals. Some of my business is generated on the golf course or over lunch with developers, lawyers, bank officials, financial counselors, and relocation specialists.
>
> I also do a lot of my work evenings, Saturdays, even Sundays. This odd-hours work is usually interviewing prospective borrowers, explaining various loan programs to them, and helping them with mortgage application forms, but sometimes I give talks at nearby community colleges, and sometimes I sit through a builder's open house to offer financing to interested buyers.
>
> I usually go to the buyers' homes or to the Realtor's office to meet and qualify the prospective borrowers and to fill out the loan applications. Then I use my office in my home to do the telephone work and additional paperwork.
>
> I love the freedom and flexibility of this job. You'd never get me into a corporate office again!

In Michigan, mortgage broker Marian Klainer maintains a small downtown office and employs a secretary and one other loan originator. "This office is a luxury," says Klainer.

I leave home stuff behind when I come here, and it costs me nothing. I own this building, so the rent from the other suite on this floor and the two on the upper floor pays all the carrying costs.

How do I build my business? Well, I advertise in the yellow pages and sometimes in the local papers, but most of my business really comes in through referrals. It'll probably sound old-fashioned, but this is the kind of business that you build in a community where you know people and you yourself are known and trusted. It takes a lot of goodwill and good service.

It also takes a lot of, well, faith. There's no incremental salary schedule, no promotions, no company benefits package. What I make is generated by me. And I never know whether next year, or even next month, will be good. Fortunately, it has been. Even with the slow economy. Maybe partly because of it. People are looking for the best deal they can get in everything, even mortgages.

In many ways, Huddleton and Klainer are typical of newly established professionals. The majority of mortgage brokerage firms, however, employ four to ten people, and some are very large. Also, life in the mortgage marketplace is not always quite as pleasant as they describe. They didn't mention the required hours of paperwork, the pressure to qualify prospective borrowers carefully because a declined loan represents lost time and income, and the constant need to develop and cultivate relationships with lenders. (Studies show that most brokers work with approximately 12 different lenders.)

In the larger mortgage brokerage firms and in most mortgage banking firms, the work that Huddleton and Klainer describe is divided among specialists. These are the many hats that the independent businessperson must wear:

*Loan originators*, also called *loan solicitors*, are the men and women in the field. They spend more time out of the office than in it and function very much like corporate sales representatives. Their job is to find qualified borrowers, take mortgage applications, and guide the borrowers through the lending process.

*Loan underwriters* evaluate borrower applications to determine if the loan is a prudent investment. They're especially attentive to property appraisals and credit reports. In the end, they stamp "approved" or "declined" on each application. They also establish overall company guidelines on risk (how much is too much, what's a good risk and what's not, and so forth). Except in times of high volume in a very brisk seller's market, underwriters work regular hours in the company office: no overtime and no weekends.

*Loan processors* and *servicing staff members* deal with the necessary paperwork. In mortgage banking firms, they also collect and record loan payments, forward payments to the mortgage holders, oversee escrow accounts for the payment of taxes and insurance, and make the necessary phone calls when payments are late.

*Office managers* supervise and coordinate all of the above. Some office managers also work as loan originators.

*Marketing staff members* are usually among the most experienced people in the company. They must know all aspects of the secondary mortgage market, including the goings-on in commercial banks, the remaining S&Ls, pension funds, Fannie Mae, institutional investors, investment bankers, and Wall Street brokerage houses. Marketing people sell the mortgages their company originated and thus bring new capital into the firm. Without them, money for originating loans would run out, and the business could not continue.

*Income property finance specialists* handle complex, big-ticket deals that are secured by income-producing real estate, such as office buildings, shopping centers, industrial parks, vacation resorts, hotels, apartment houses, and so on. They usually recommend a specific deal to an investor or investment group. The investor puts up an agreed-upon amount of money on specified terms secured by a specified property. The income property finance specialist then arranges construction financing and, near the end of the project, arranges long-term financing. Sometimes income property finance specialists arrange joint ventures, and sometimes the mortgage banker firm will also manage the property created by the joint venture.

## The Money

Mortgage brokers are middlemen and most of them don't get paid unless a deal is closed. Brokers who place loans servicing released with institutional lenders are paid a certain percentage of the loan value they place. The percentage is expressed in *basis points*, one point being 0.001 (one-tenth of 1 percent) of the face value of the loan. Sometimes mortgage brokers also collect a small, one-time service fee from the borrower.

Figures in the 1992 National Association of Mortgage Brokers (NAMB) Mortgage Broker Industry Study indicate average estimated earnings of $75,000 per $10 million of production (originated mortgages). By this standard, a mortgage broker who originated $30 million would have an income of $225,000.

Mortgage bankers work more like a retail trade store whose product is money. When selling home mortgages, they begin by using either their own capital or short-term borrowings to make mortgage loans to home buyers. Several of these loans are then grouped together for sale as packages to outside investors, usually large institutions. The proceeds of that sale are then used to pay salaries and expenses and to replenish the supply of money for new home mortgages as the cycle starts again. Even after the loans are sold, however, mortgage bankers continue to collect fees for servicing the loans.

The annual incomes of the specialists in mortgage banking companies vary widely by job and geographic location. Most servicing staff members are paid a salary, which averaged in the mid $20,000s in 1992. Underwriters are also usually on salary, but their annual incomes are generally higher than those of loan processors. The salaries of marketing specialists are not affected by volume or based on commission, and they are higher still. Loan originators and income property finance specialists are paid by different schedules in different companies, but the plans usually include a minimum salary comparable to the loan processor's salary with added commissions and/or bonuses. Company executives are usually paid a salary with a potential bonus based on profits.

A career booklet published by the Mortgage Bankers Association of America states, "Mortgage banking is generally a well-paid profession, with strong possibilities for very substantial rewards. Some positions, such as that of loan originator, receive commissions over and above minimum salaries that can allow talented people to earn more than the presidents of their companies."

## The People

Although the job is immersed in numbers, selling money is people-oriented work. A mortgage broker or banker is part counselor, part manager, part accountant, part hunter, and part hawker. Despite the power advantage generated by knowledge of the financial marketplace, the mortgage professional must work diligently at selling the available loan products and at developing the trust of the public. Both of these tasks depend on the reactions of other people to what he or she says and does.

Edith McConville, a vice-president at First Federal Savings Bank of Florida who is responsible for training the bank's entire staff of loan originators, says, "The best loan originators have a combination of salesmanship and technical skills. They work at selling the product, but they also take on the responsibility of asking the tough questions, the questions that make or break a loan, like 'What is the origin of the down payment money?' The worst loans, the ones that get declined most often, are brought to the bank by the loan originators who think of themselves as great salesmen."

Beyond your interaction with borrowers, your success in mortgage banking or mortgage brokerage will depend on your interaction with peers and supervisors. Your peers in this career are your co-workers, your competitors, local real estate agents, employees in local financial institutions, builders and developers, accountants, architects, lawyers, and other community professionals. Research shows that referrals are the chief source of new customers, and referrals are the direct result of goodwill. Bear in mind that only a small part of the work of selling mortgages takes place in the office. Building this career is a 24-hour-a-day job that depends heavily on interaction within the community.

With the exception of large firms with office managers and a corporate hierarchy, supervision in mortgage banking and mortgage brokerage is often about as impersonal as IRS supervision of your tax return. In comparison to banking, insurance, and real estate, mortgage banking and mortgage brokerage is a very lightly regulated industry. Some states (Alaska, South Dakota, Louisiana, and Vermont as of this writing) have no regulation at all. And even the licensing and/or net-worth requirements in the toughest states (Illinois, New Jersey, New York, and Virginia) are not so restrictive as to discourage the formation of new mortgage banking and brokerage firms.

In addition to state regulatory supervision, there are trade groups in most states. Members in these groups agree to adhere to their group's code of ethics and to abide by its mediation. Thus, in effect, they agree to supervision by peers. But in the end, the real, day-to-day, hour-by-hour supervision in the business of selling mortgages is self-supervision.

## Getting In

There are no specific education requirements for a career in mortgage banking or mortgage brokerage. Most large firms and most trade groups recommend a four-year degree with course work in finance, economics, accounting, and real estate in addition to well-developed writing and communication skills. Courses or training in engineering are a useful background for construction financing.

However, on-the-job experience in banking, real estate sales, appraisal, negotiating, or law could easily stand in for the recommended college degree and could open the door to an entry-level job in a large firm. Once in, movement from one specialty to another is not uncommon.

State regulations for entering the profession vary widely. In those states with low requirements, there are small license fees, few if any compliance exams, no testing or educational standards, and no net-worth requirements. States with moderate requirements have somewhat larger license fees and may require surety bonds, periodic audits, and testing. States with high requirements impose larger license fees, more costly and/or more frequent exams, annual filings, and minimum net-worth standards.

Overall, regulation of the industry is relatively recent. Most laws and rules have been adopted since 1987, and being new, they are subject to change. Currently, there are movements afoot for stricter controls in several states, but these efforts are being opposed by trade organization–sponsored lobbies. Regulators from 12 states have established a group, the American Association of Residential Mortgage Regulators, to work toward national uniformity in license laws. You can get information on your state's requirements by calling your state banking commission.

For those with extensive community networks in real estate and banking, the job of self-employed mortgage broker may be the first step to building a multimillion-dollar company. Cash start-up requirements are considerably less than for most other businesses. Just under 25 percent of the nation's mortgage brokers operate out of their homes, and 31 percent have three or fewer employees. The median net worth of mortgage broker firms in 1992 was $75,000, which in many cases included ownership of the building that housed the firm.

## Is This for You?

If you are impatient, dependent on routine, anxious, or unmotivated, dealing in mortgages is not for you. The career calls for individuals who are conscientious, self-starting, analytical, insightful, persevering, creative, and flexible. A healthy self-image doesn't hurt either.

The easiest way to get the basic training for the career is to work as a loan originator for a large commercial or savings bank or a large mortgage banker company. While learning the ropes and developing your own network of referral contacts, you'll enjoy some degree of job security and the usual employment benefits. If you choose to enter the profession by starting your own business as a mortgage broker, however, you should be aware of the risks. According to the 1992 NAMB study, 20 percent of all new businesses never make it through the first year of operation, and 50 percent close within the first five years. Those that make it past the first five years, however, seem to do very well.

Both mortgage brokerage and mortgage banking are much more prevalent in and near large cities than in rural areas. According to NAMB, the 20 states with the largest number of mortgage brokers are (in order by highest number first) California, Florida, New York, New Jersey, Connecticut, Maryland, Arizona, Pennsylvania, Illinois, Massachusetts, Michigan, Virginia, Texas, Colorado, Ohio, Hawaii, Washington, Missouri, North Carolina, and Nevada.

The outlook for this career during the 1990s is quite favorable, provided that federal legislation does not impose unmanageable restrictions and licensing requirements. Because the increasing competition and complexity of the mortgage marketplace make mortgage shopping an anxiety trip for people already emotionally exhausted from the house hunt, home buyers are becoming more and more inclined to seek out the services of a mortgage broker or mortgage banker. In other words, consumer perception of the career is increasingly positive.

On the supplier's side, the demise of the S&Ls and the resulting tightening of lending regulations has changed the mortgage marketplace. According to the 1992 NAMB study titled *The Nation's Mortgage Brokers*, retail lenders are switching to wholesale activities to lower expenses (fewer employees and fewer branch offices) and to increase returns. They are finding that the economics of buying loans from mortgage brokers and mortgage bankers is more favorable than marketing and originating them directly. Thus, the perception of mortgage brokers or mortgage bankers is positive in the wholesale market also.

With increasing demand both wholesale (banks and lenders) and retail (borrowers), the business of selling money should prove a challenging and rewarding career well into the new millennium. Today's and tomorrow's mortgage marketplace and its new technology favor specialization, and the broker or banker is a specialist in demand.

## For More Information

A booklet titled *Careers in Mortgage Banking* is available from the Mortgage Bankers Association of America (see Appendix I for listing). A study titled *The Nation's Mortgage Brokers* and a profile of the career are available from the National Association of Mortgage Brokers (see Appendix I for listing).

The NAMB also recommends the following books:

*The Handbook of Mortgage Banking: A Guide to the Secondary Mortgage Market*, by James M. Kinney and Richard T. Garrigan (New York: Dow Jones-Irwin, 1985).

*The Loan Officer's Handbook*, edited by William J. Korsvik and Charles O. Meilburg (New York: Dow Jones-Irwin, 1986).

*Real Estate Finance*, 6th ed., by John P. Wiedemer (Englewood Cliffs, NJ: Prentice-Hall, 1987).

Edith McConville recommends this one:

*Marketing and Selling Mortgage Services*, by David Hershman (Chicago: Probus Publishing, 1992).

# The World of Shopping Center Management

Some can remember their first visit to an enclosed shopping center and the wondrous experience it was, back in the sleepy 1950s or early 1960s. For others, heading for these suburban meccas is practically the only major shopping style they have known. Need a shirt? Eyeglasses? Some cash from the ATM? Want to catch a movie? Eat Chinese food or pizza or tacos? It's all there in the 100 or more services and shops, plus entertainment center, that make up the mall.

Shopping centers are no doubt a factor that contributed to the death of downtown and central city shopping areas, but in the ongoing change of the nation's landscape, they did meet the needs of the masses of Americans who headed for the suburbs after World War II. Today, the opening of a new mall rarely makes news. A greater number of shops than ever before, glass elevators, unusual promotions, multiplex theaters—we've seen it all.

Well, almost all. In August 1992, the opening of the huge Mall of America in Bloomington, Minnesota, a suburb of Minneapolis, managed to make most of us pause for a moment of genuine admiration. Here is a mall with 4.2 million square feet planned (the country's larger superregional malls have 1 million-plus square feet), 78 acres, nearly 400 stores, and an entertainment complex. When Mall of America is complete, the Del Amo Fashion Center in Torrance, California, slips down to second largest mall in the country, boasting 3 million square feet.

According to the International Council of Shopping Centers, there are nearly 38,000 shopping centers in this country, including strip malls. Strip malls consist of small service shops, usually anchored by a supermarket. Some smaller shopping centers, known as power malls, are now built around so-called category killers—enormous specialty stores like Home Depot, Price Club, and Toys 'R' Us that offer buyers deep discounts. Other small centers operate on the factory outlet theme, with clusters of stores also promising low prices. All of these centers run under 400,000 square feet, according to groupings within the trade.

Regional and superregional malls range from 400,000 to more than 1 million square feet. These usually have four to six department stores serving as anchors.

The only megamall in this country is the Mall of America. Its only competition is the megamall in Edmonton, Alberta. The Mall of America was developed by Melvin Simon & Associates, a U.S. firm, and Triple Five Corporation, the Canadian developer of the Edmonton shopping center.

John Wheeler, manager of Mall of America, has been associated with Melvin Simon for nearly a decade. He explains, using the corporate team-player *we*, how the choice of mall manager was determined at Simon:

> We wanted someone who was an experienced Simon person. Every company has just a little different approach to how they manage their real estate. We have found the more responsible the position, the more we want someone who has our philosophy.
>
> We also wanted to take a fresh look at managing Mall of America. We didn't just want to assume that it was a regular mall times four. We considered it a unique property and didn't want someone bound by old ways of doing things. We also needed a good manager—the mall has a staff of 450 persons. I knew mall management and had been involved in special projects and task forces out in the field, which was actually just 10 miles from the office, so I was chosen.

Supervising strip malls for the corporation that owns several of them is usually done from office headquarters. Managing a regional or superregional mall is an on-site position, and that is what we will cover in this chapter.

John P. Richley, director of operations for The Cafaro Company, a firm of mall owners, developers, and managers based in Youngstown, Ohio, notes, "A lot of people in this country—and me in fact before I got into mall management—don't realize this business exists. People walking through a mall concourse have no idea of the behind-the-scenes work that goes on. There is a true career here in managing a shopping center."

## The Work

In mall management, you start small, graduate to a bigger mall, and then move on to one that is larger still. Alice D. Ballenger, manager of a midsize mall in a southern city, is an example of the relative beginner. Like most careers in real estate, shopping center management is not what little boys and girls say they want to do when they grow up. Also like most real estate careers, one arrives here from employment arenas that run a wide gamut. Ballenger's path is typical, so let's follow her first steps to mall management.

Raised in a small town in the South, she left college before graduation to assist her father with his auto dealership. He died a year later, and at the age of 21 she secured a real estate license and moved into time-share, condominium, and land sales locally. A few years later it was back to autos, this time as business manager for a local Chevrolet dealership. Still not satisfied with her career but with limited choices in her hometown area, Ballenger headed for a local branch of a national employment agency, where she was hired as a counselor.

While there she noticed an opening for someone to handle temporary leasing at a 700,000-square-foot mall in the area. Temp leasing, as it is known, involves kiosks and carts throughout a center as well as the "in-line" space—the regular mall shops, which are let on a temporary or seasonal basis. Temp leasing agents usually do not need a real estate license, and indeed by this time Ballenger's license had lapsed.

She was hired based on her varied retailing experience. After two years she was made assistant manager of the mall, which was owned by Bramalea Centers, a Dallas-based firm with eight shopping centers around the United States. The firm is part of Bramalea Limited, which is headquartered in Canada, where it owns and manages another 30 or so centers.

Her duties as assistant manager included a continuation of temp leasing, and it was not long before Ballenger felt she was ready to manage a mall. When she learned of an opening in Durango, Colorado, for manager of a 250,000-square-foot

Bramalea mall, she applied and won the slot. She would be both manager and marketing director. (Larger malls consider these to be two different positions and sometimes have a separate position for promotion director as well.)

"Basically I cleaned house there," she recalls of her stay in Colorado. "There were maintenance and other concerns. When I reached my goals and the mall was doing well, I ready for the next step."

The next rung on the ladder for a relatively new mall manager is usually a larger, perhaps plusher, mall. For Ballenger, the move was to a larger mall, but not a more upscale one. She learned that Bramalea was looking for someone to manage its 700,000-square-foot mall in a city of 800,000 near her hometown. She would be going to a mall more than twice the size of the Durango mall, and she would be close to home.

There was just one thing, however, that some might consider a snag. This was a property with some problems. A few large tenants had moved out, either because of bankruptcies or mergers within their companies. A popular restaurant had bowed out too. Changing demographics and the age of the mall contributed to its somewhat faded look. It had begun as a strip center built in 1957 and expanded in 1959. The enclosed mall was constructed in 1967, with some freestanding buildings added in 1975. The head office was working on resolving the difficulties and making the mall viable again. Indeed, there was a major renovation program on the boards, and inside the management office was an elaborate diorama. Some approvals were needed, and more financial details had to be worked out, so workers were not exactly digging in yet. In the meantime, a manager was needed to replace the current director, who was heading for another city, following *his* career path.

This mall, Ballenger recalls, offered a challenge. She wanted the assignment, and she won it. At this writing, she has been in the position for two months, supervising a staff of 26, most of them working in security and maintenance. She has rented a few vacant spaces, some on her own and some in cooperation with the home office in Dallas, which goes after larger national tenants through its leasing agent. Ballenger has not been handed the responsibility of filling up vacant retail space. The corporate headquarters of most developer/manager companies handle major leasing, especially anchor stores, although the on-site mall manager often rents to local mom-and-pop tenants and small regional chains.

Ballenger's principal responsibilities are to collect rents and to keep tenants relatively contented. What's a typical day like? "Let's see," she says, ticking off the previous day's activities.

> I met with an engineer about tearing down a wall so a tenant can expand into more space. I had a problem with a part of the roof. I talked with a staff member over some concerns there. I had an assignment of a lease, where one person wanted to sell and we had a buyer, so we signed the lease over to the new owner.
>
> I met with another tenant who wants to expand into a larger store here, so I have to work up some costs for him. I talked with a tenant about a sign we have to approve for his store. I made arrangements with four people to set up a temporary booth. Oh, and it was the ninth of the month, so I looked over our listings for rent delinquencies.
>
> Another tenant left yesterday, and I have to collect the keys. And I met with two tenants in one store who want to terminate their lease, which we are not able to do. That's a kind of hard thing to do at the end of a day.

Ballenger adds that she receives about 25 phone calls daily. She also tries to walk through the property every day.

The rewards, she says, are "small victories." One of her pet peeves is "lease lines," the invisible boundaries in front of stores beyond which merchants may not display their goods for sale. There was quite a lot of overstepping those limits when Ballenger took the helm at her center. After asking the offenders to rein in their displays, Ballenger says, "I wondered if everyone was still going to be out in the common area the next day. But only two were, and I talked to them and we worked it out. I've had a number of tenants tell me they're impressed with what's happened since I came. That's the good part too." Her principal difficulty is finding time: "There just isn't enough of it to do all I need to do. I wish I had a really top-notch assistant manager."

Besides their principal responsibilities of collecting rents and keeping tenants relatively happy, mall managers have a number of other tasks. They must also manage the mall budget; work to control the growing number of crime incidents in malls and mall parking lots; become known in the area in which the mall is situated (besides in the retail community); see that windows of vacant mall shops are decorated so that no negative signals are sent to mall shoppers and supervise individual store and overall interior renovations. Mall managers must deal with bomb scares and must know what type of asphalt should be put down on the new parking lot. More than one has come up with innovative ways to rent unused space, such as subdividing a store into small concessions. Every day is busy, and every day brings a wide variety of challenges to address—although those who see the hole and not the donut might say a wide variety of problems to solve!

## The Money

As a mall manager, you will be salaried, so you will not feel the panic—or, as some might see it, the exhilaration—of working on a commissions-only basis.

Huntress Real Estate Executive Search, in Kansas City, Missouri, compiled a report about compensation in the industry, which should give you some idea of salaries. According to their 1992 report, managers of regional malls earned from $59,500 to $82,300. Managers of strip malls drew $47,600 to $68,000. Marketing directors earned $46,800 to $66,500, and promotion directors pulled in $36,200 to $53,100.

Although malls and their managers have had their problems over the last few years, salaries have so far not been affected. The Huntress survey found that from 1986 to 1991, shopping center executives' compensation increased 26.3 percent. During that same time, the Consumer Price Index rose 22.9 percent. Keep in mind, of course, that 1986 to around 1989 were boom years for the economy in general and that "executives" includes the upper-level home-office positions.

Starting out means lower compensation, of course. Ballenger says, "I took a big cut from the auto industry to start with temp leasing, although it was a salary in the 20s." Assistant managers can expect similar pay, although salaries depend on the size of the mall and the developer/manager's pay scale. Because one is salaried in all these positions, there is a full range of benefits and perks.

## The People

Besides the mall manager, larger malls also have an assistant manager, perhaps a temporary leasing agent, a marketing director, and sometimes a promotion director.

Some say that the position of marketing director is not on the career path to management. It is, they say, for those who have experience in writing or public relations. The marketing director usually handles cooperative advertising programs with all tenants as well as special promotions and sales.

In very large malls, marketing slots are heavy-duty work. The opinion of some that these jobs are not on the management track comes as news to some marketing professionals, such as Richley of The Cafaro Company, who is a marketing booster. "You *can* make the transition to manager from marketing," he says. "Everything a manager does sends a marketing signal. Also, you'd better know the field because as mall manager you're going to be charged with management of the marketing director."

Within the regional mall are a number of other employees, the bulk of whom fall under the heading of maintenance and safety crews. The mall manager oversees these personnel as well as the small office support staff. Overall, the staff of a regional or superregional mall can number 50 to 100 or more employees.

Mall managers answer to regional managers and sometimes work with others in the home office, such as leasing agents. There can be stress, of course, in keeping large numbers of people happy, including mall shoppers, one's own staff, and the home office.

What comes next after serving well at one of the nation's larger malls? You might move into a regional vice-president slot with your company, overseeing a number of shopping centers. There are usually other positions in the home office at the vice-president level, sometimes segueing from shopping centers to another of the corporation's realty interests.

There are those who feel on-site mall management is not a lifelong career. You burn out after six or seven years at one mall, they claim. You might get too close to your tenants and forget who you are working for. Also, the job means constantly moving for each promotion, possibly creating the problem of the "trailing spouse." Ballenger married while still working in her hometown. Her husband is in sales and was able to find work in Durango, which is a pretty tough job market because it is essentially a vacation area. After two months in the city where the couple now lives, he is still job hunting, but neither spouse anticipates a serious problem with his eventually finding a satisfactory position. Ballenger's husband supports her career and its movement around the country. Some spouses might not.

After several years running a mall in one locale, managers who do not wish to move again can generally exploit the extensive networking they have done over the years and the high profile they have maintained in their community to find work at a comparable level with another employer in another industry. Being manager of an upscale mall does have a certain cachet in area business, banking, and real estate circles.

Ballenger notes that five of the eight Bramalea malls in the United States are managed by women. There is still a plurality of male names on vice-presidents' doors at major mall companies, but as women rise through the ranks, one might expect that will change.

As mentioned earlier, the professional association for mall managers is the International Council of Shopping Centers, based in New York City. Some 95 percent of all mall managers belong to the ICSC.

The professional designation, offered through the ICSC, is Certified Shopping Center Manager (CSM). Not all managers can credit CSM to their names, but at some point most do work for those coveted initials. To qualify for the CSM examination, which is offered yearly at a location determined by the ICSC, the applicant must have been actively engaged in shopping center management as a manager for four years. The council also offers Certified Marketing Director (CMD) designation, which is awarded after fulfilling ICSC requirements.

## Getting In

If you are interested in becoming a mall manager, you have several options.

An undergraduate or graduate degree in business, with several shopping center–related courses, certainly helps. Youngstown State University in Ohio offers such a program. It was suggested to the school several years ago by representatives of two large mall developers in the area: The Cafaro Company and Edward J. DeBartolo Corporation, both of which continue to maintain contact with the school's management program (and hire some of its graduates!).

"I look for some construction knowledge," says Richley of The Cafaro Company, in talking about manager requirements, "or at least an understanding of the terminology. Applicants should have at least some marketing experience or education from a marketing point of view. And, of course, some retail background."

Aren't strengths in three different areas a little hard to come by? Richley says no. "You can call just about any store manager across the country and find many of them who may not have thought of themselves as proper candidates, but after you spend some time with them, you—and they—realize they know more than they thought. The unique thing about this job is that it is so diverse that you need to have some knowledge about a lot of different subjects."

Shopping center managers come from a variety of other careers. One was a restaurant manager; one was manager of a small boutique; another was a department store buyer; one worked her way up from a position of temporary secretary at the mall. Many start, as Ballenger did, with temporary leasing or step into assistant manager's slots.

The ICSC's special week-long "Institutes" are invaluable for the beginner. The ICSC offers them a few times a year in different parts of the country, and all-day meetings are offered even more frequently, usually on one subject. At these one-day sessions, you will learn a good deal about the field and will have an opportunity to do some important networking too.

You can also apply directly to large mall owners/developers. They are listed below in order of decreasing size:

JMB Retail Properties Co.
900 N. Michigan Ave.
Chicago, IL 60611
Telephone (312) 440-4800

Melvin Simon & Associates
Merchants Plaza
P.O. Box 7033
Indianapolis, IN 46207
Telephone (317) 636-1600

Edward J. DeBartolo Corporation
7620 Market St.
Youngstown, OH 44513
Telephone (216) 758-7292

## Is This for You?

Besides strong management skills, you will need to be temperamentally suited to this position. As mentioned, you must be willing to travel to further your career. You also need a thick skin. You cannot flinch in telling a tenant, "No, we will not give you a rent reduction." You must be willing to pursue delinquencies, move outs, and rent raises, and you must be able to handle feuding tenants—and that is not to mention the problems that will occur in your own office with your staff.

Not all of your 150 or so tenants are going to love you all the time. If their sales are down, for whatever reason, guess where they are going to vent their displeasure? "If you're always worried about everybody liking you, don't even think about this business," says Ballenger. "It isn't a popularity contest."

Richley adds, "A director needs to be extremely resilient and flexible and willing to work in excess of the typical 40-hour week because malls are open 72 hours a week. You have to be able to track the trends in real estate and in retailing and customer reactions. Wearing all those different hats is not easy." And, notes one mall observer, there are 17 attorneys back in the home office waiting to see how you handle things!

In terms of employment, the overall mall picture has become a little hazy over the last several years, following the boom years of the previous two decades. In terms of development, the ICSC reported only 471 shopping centers under construction in 1992, compared with 565 the year before, 985 in 1990, and 1,510 in 1989. Melvin Simon & Associates, for one, planned to open only 10 new centers in 1992, compared to 80 just five years ago. Obviously, they are not alone in cutbacks. Although some large malls are doing quite nicely, the recession of the early 1990s has hit others. Some older malls, constructed 30 years ago, are now outdated and will take sizable amounts of money to be upgraded. That is money some developer/owners do not have or are not willing to spend.

Some in the industry believe that there is less mall traffic these days. They say busy—and cash-strapped—two-career families are heading for factory outlets or discount houses either in small malls or in no mall configuration at all. Fewer seem to have the time, mall analysts say, to spend in sprawling malls, where there are few, if any, discount houses anyway. These changes in the way Americans shop might affect future mall construction and the financial success of existing malls into the next decade.

Developers and would-be developers face other concerns. The bankruptcies and mergers of a number of department stores over the last several years left a smaller number of prospective tenants for malls. Financing for new projects might be difficult, and land-use restrictions can affect where new malls can be built.

Overall, it is difficult to predict the future of employment in the shopping center management industry. More than one observer has wondered about Mall of America: Is it the end of an era for big malls, or will it prove to be the beginning of a new one? Mall shoppers and, needless to say, mall managers are cheering for the latter path. Stay tuned.

## For More Information

*Carpenter's Shopping Center Management*, edited by Robert J. Flynn, CSM, a classic in the field, is available from ICSC for $89.00 for nonmembers. See Appendix I for ICSC's address.

| CHAPTER | Take a Look under |
|---|---|
| 8 | the Rug |

*The Home Inspector and the
Home Inspection Company*

There's a grandfather in Connecticut who claims that a home inspector ruined his best shirt. It happened while he was visiting his son, who had sold his house and was about to move to another state.

This grandfather had a backache and didn't go along with the rest of the family, all of whom wanted to be out during the inspection. So he sat resolutely at the kitchen table while the inspector and the buyers went through every cubic foot of interior space. He nodded stiffly when they said "Good-bye" and watched them exit through the sliding glass door.

Relieved that they were gone, Grandpa picked up his coffee cup and was about to take a long, deep drink when he glimpsed the inspector jumping up and down on the far corner of the deck. The old man bolted up faster than he thought he could, and with hot black coffee soaking into the front of his shirt, he charged outside.

"What the hell do you think you're doing?" he shouted.

"I'm testing the soundness of the deck construction," replied the inspector. "It seems to be real good."

The old man glared, said nothing, and went back inside. When his family returned home, he told them the "incredible" story of the "idiot" home inspector. "I can't believe people really pay money for that!" he repeated again and again.

Well, they do. More people are hiring home inspectors now than ever before. Virtually an unknown profession in the 1960s, the American Society of Home Inspectors (ASHI) had counted 5,754 home inspection firms in the United States and 457 in Canada by the early 1990s. And what's more, most of the people who hire home inspectors feel that they get excellent value for their money.

Grandpa's attitude toward the home inspector is typical of several common misunderstandings of the profession. Many home sellers fear and resent the home inspector as judge and jury of the sale; many home buyers expect the inspector to be a combination of Superman (who can see through walls) and a professional engineer equipped with the latest in systems and structure testing technology. None of it is true.

A house doesn't pass or fail inspection, and no well-trained inspector would either recommend or advise against a home purchase. The home inspector's job is to report on the condition and soundness of the structure and working systems. The report is usually based on what can be seen without disturbing, defacing, or disrupting any part of the property or its working systems and on what can be tested using the controls that any homeowner might use while living in the house. Home inspectors don't take anything apart, and most of them don't use mathematical, technical, or chemical testing devices.

## The Work

If you want to be seen regularly in Ralph Lauren blazers and gray flannel slacks, this is not the career for you. Home inspectors usually have a fondness for the soft texture of much-washed jeans, and they definitely don't mind getting their hands dirty. There is a part of the job, however, where blazers *are* appropriate.

The typical workweek of a neophyte home inspector has three major components: marketing the service, doing the inspections, and writing the reports.

Marketing is the part where blazers are appropriate. Especially at the outset of their careers, inspectors must convince other professionals in the real estate marketplace that their service is competent, ethical, and valuable. Because referrals in the business most often come from relocation counselors, Realtors, mortgage brokers, and lawyers, time must be allocated to maintaining an extensive network of local real estate professionals. The most common network-building tactics are personal visits to offices (sometimes dropping off brochures, calendars, magnets, and so on), luncheon meetings, and shared recreational activities, such as golf, tennis, or boating.

Some home inspectors also build their business by making

contact with the public directly. They exhibit at local home shows, and they develop programs for presentation at local adult schools, community colleges, corporate conferences, conventions, and club meetings, such as the Newcomers or Welcome Wagon.

As the home inspector becomes known in an area, more jobs come in, and a greater portion of each week is spent in the process of inspecting. This is the part where jeans are appropriate. The average home inspection takes two to three hours. The work usually includes climbing a ladder to look at the roof, flashings, gutters, and drain pipes, and it may include peering through the dust and spiderwebs of an attic or crouching in the dirt of a crawl space beneath the house. The home inspector will open faucets, flush toilets, run the dishwasher, test the plumbing, waste disposal, heating, and air conditioning systems, look for signs of water seepage in the basement, test the oven and stove, note the electrical service, check the electrical switches and outlets, and examine moldings and door jambs for signs of settling. In the best of circumstances, a good deal of time will be spent pointing out, explaining, and discussing components of the house with the prospective buyer.

The third part of the job, writing the reports on inspected homes, once took many work hours, often late into the night. The development and availability of the personal computer has changed that, however. Information written out on a clipboard during the inspection can now be keyed into the proper spaces on the computer screen, and a report can then be printed in a fraction of the time it once took to type just the first page or two. Some home inspectors even use portable computers as their clipboards. They can print their reports on printers in their trucks within minutes after leaving the property.

Among the tools commonly carried by home inspectors are pencils, paper, a clipboard, ladders, a magnet, ropes, an outlet tester, screwdrivers, a ruler or tape measure, binoculars, matches to test venting, a mirror, an oven thermometer, and probably most important, a high-powered flashlight. Some inspectors take a camera and sometimes a tape recorder along, and some even take a portable word processor into the home and print out the report on the spot. (They also get paid on the spot.)

Virtually all inspectors also bring along a pair of coveralls, boots, gloves, a hat, and a face mask, all to be used if needed. And although it's possible to drive one's Alfa Romeo or BMW to luncheons and meetings, most home inspectors drive a small truck or van to inspection assignments in order to accommodate the necessary ladder, tools, and take-alongs.

If you choose this career, you won't have an assigned, color-coordinated work cubicle or a numbered parking space. Your working hours will be irregular and usually the direct result of your motivation, planning, and drive. Rarely will you be required to leave your bed in time to see the sun rise, but fairly often you'll find yourself spending some evening and weekend hours at your job. Although you'll probably enjoy the flexibility of your day, you'll also need to pay particular attention to scheduling because nothing starts a home inspection out in a more negative tone than an inspector who is late.

Because most home inspection work is dependent on home sales, your career will probably have a seasonal rhythm similar to that of a real estate sales agent. Spring, early summer, and early fall are usually the busiest times. There is rarely much work in December, and many home inspectors take their vacations in January and February. July and August are slower than spring months but active enough to keep the inspector's golf dates within the amateur category.

## The Money

"Unlike real estate agents, the income of home inspectors doesn't hit peaks and valleys in tandem with the state of the economy," says Alan Carson of Carson, Dunlop & Associates, a firm with three offices in and around Toronto. "Business is more even because more people order home inspections in a slow buyer's market. There may be fewer houses sold, but a larger percentage are being inspected.

"Also," adds Carson, "this is a genuinely growing industry. There are more home inspections being done every year in the United States and Canada."

In a 1991 survey, ASHI, the oldest and largest of the national home inspector trade organizations, found that the mean income of home inspectors was $48,000 a year. Some members working part-time, however, reported incomes as low as $6,000 a year, while other well-established inspectors reported incomes in excess of $90,000.

The average fee charged for a home inspection in the United

States is $250. That figure varies, however, by geographic area and according to the size and style of the home being inspected.

In one-person or mom-and-pop firms, the inspector, of course, collects and keeps the entire fee. In more corporatelike firms consisting of one or more principals who employ several inspectors, payment for work is determined by agreement between the owner of the firm and the employed inspector. Carson, Dunlop & Associates pays its inspectors an annual salary, disbursed over the course of the year. Some firms pay their inspectors by the hour or by the assignment.

Besides collecting fees for inspections ordered by home buyers, some home inspectors augment their incomes by acting as independent contractors for agencies or large companies. For example, Real Estate Support Services, the largest firm in the United States doing corporate relocation inspections, maintains a roster of approved independent contractors in the United States, Canada, and Puerto Rico. The company pays a set fee for each assigned inspection.

Work is also available through other housing-related employers. Leroy N. Smith of Fort Worth, Texas, for example, is an independent home inspector who works exclusively on assignments for the Federal Housing Administration (FHA). Home inspection assignments can also come from the Resolution Trust Corporation, other federal government agencies, municipal governments, and occasionally mortgage lenders.

## The People

With a list of specific tasks that includes climbing ladders and poking about under the kitchen sink, the job of a home inspector certainly requires some physical labor. But nothing is produced and nothing is changed as a result of the work. The career is a people-serving business.

Knowledge of its technical aspects is essential, but interpersonal skills are equally important in determining success. A home inspector spends very few working hours alone. "At work" usually means being with a client at an inspection or networking in the real estate marketplace. A sincere smile, a firm handshake, and good listening skills are tools as valuable as a ladder and a flashlight.

"The dynamics of home buying and selling are stressful, and

home inspection is right up there at peak stress time," says Vera Hollander Wadler, a spokesperson for the American Society of Home Inspectors. "It's very important that a home inspector be able to establish rapport with his client. At the same time, the inspector must avoid antagonizing both the home seller and the real estate agent. Communication skills must be excellent, and tact and honesty as character traits demand ratings of 10!"

For those with good communication skills, working with customers is one of the rewards of the profession. Frank Conder, and independent home inspector in Texas with more than 25 years in the business, says, "Ninety-eight percent of the people are great! You know, I usually make the least money but the 'best bucks' when I do inspections for first-time buyers. They are always anxious, and it's so satisfying to be able to help them."

On the other hand, the home inspector's desire to be helpful and appreciated can sometimes be a source of stress in this career. Despite more than ten years of successful inspections to her credit, Cheryll Brown still sometimes worries that she may have missed something, especially something concealed by a wily seller. In addition, inspectors who are hired to work for corporate relocation companies are sometimes bombarded with complaints and disclaimers from sellers, who see home inspection reports as part of the home appraisal done in the process of selling to the company.

## Getting In

So you still want to be a home inspector? Well, hang out a shingle!

That's all it takes in every state in the United States—except Texas—and all of Canada. Texas is almost as tough in licensing home inspectors as it is on real estate agents. To qualify as an apprentice inspector, 90 classroom hours in core real estate inspection courses, as defined by the state, must be completed. Then the apprentice inspector must be supervised by a licensed inspector on a minimum of 25 inspections over the course of at least 90 days. Once these requirements are met, the candidate goes on to the intermediate step: inspector-in-training.

If you live in Texas of if you'd like to know more about the licensing laws there (after all, other states might follow suit), write to Texas Real Estate Commission Office of Home Inspection, P.O. Box 12188, Austin, Texas 78711-2188.

Although there are currently no licensing requirements elsewhere, most home inspectors come into the job from backgrounds in home construction or repair. The most common type of home inspection business today is the mom-and-pop shop in which the husband does the inspections and the wife answers the phone and does all the paperwork. Start-up costs for such a business can be as little as $10,000, including a personal computer or word processor and a second-hand truck or van. Annual overhead is minimal because most home inspectors have an in-home office (which has certain tax benefits) and advertise only in the yellow pages of their local phone books. And because this is a service industry, there is no costly inventory to maintain.

Independent home inspectors sometimes hook into large national inspection firms that do corporate relocation. However, these firms usually require rather extensive experience and demonstrated competence before taking on a subcontractor. The independent must also conform to the inspection practices and procedures of the firm, including the use of standardized company forms. The pay structure for inspection subcontracting is something like working for a temporary employment agency: The large firm collects a certain fee from the client and then pays the worker a fee for the job (less than is collected).

Even if you are starting up a one-person business, it's not necessary to feel isolated in this career. There are numerous regional and national trade associations with a wide range of membership standards. Be selective. Some of these groups allow the use of their logo (which might include the phrase *certified home inspector*) to everyone who pays dues, but they offer little else. Others are local "fellowship" groups where a neophyte inspector can talk shop and often pick up some pointers. The largest and most prestigious North American trade association, ASHI, has rather stringent standards for membership. Successful applicants must have completed at least 250 paid professional inspections, and members must take at least 40 hours of continuing education credits over each two-year period. Membership benefits include a network of regional associations, numerous training and technical seminars, the availability of errors-and-omissions insurance, and an active public relations campaign.

As in almost every other business, growth in the home inspection industry has stimulated the growth of franchises and large corporatelike firms. Both of these business styles offer a means of getting into the career for individuals who feel "not quite ready to go it alone."

Most of the larger firms have education and training requirements, even though nothing is required by law. Carson, Dunlop & Associates in Toronto, for example, hires only graduate engineers to work as home inspectors. Then they require a training program of three to four months before the employee is allowed to do an inspection alone. Other firms prefer that a job applicant have experience and/or formal education in home construction and maintenance.

Large franchises, such as Amerispec, HouseMaster, and The Building Inspector, can provide novices with the tools necessary for success. They offer start-up and ongoing counseling, a variety of training and education programs, policies and procedures manuals, inspection forms and computer programs, billing and record-keeping forms, volume discounts on supplies and other purchases, legal advice, franchise-name advertising, a widely recognized and professionally designed logo, public relations services, group errors-and-omissions and liability insurance, group health-care plans, and a referral network.

But as you would expect, all these services don't come for nothing, as the saying goes. You must buy into a franchise, and it would be difficult to do that today for less than $15,000. Also, every franchise collects a percentage of the income of each of its members, sometimes called a royalty. Some franchises will help a prospective member to get financing for the necessary start-up costs.

Besides start-up help and management training for the home handyman or the housing construction professional who would be a home inspector, franchising also offers a means of getting into the business for men and women who have little or no knowledge of home construction and maintenance. "Some of our most successful offices are run by people with marketing and sales backgrounds," says Kenneth Austin, chairman of HouseMaster of America. "They're excellent at selling the service, maintaining networks, and managing the business details. We teach them what the business needs and what a home inspector needs to know. They hire other people to do the actual inspection work, and the franchise trains those individuals at our national training center."

## Is This for You?

If you choose to make your living as a home inspector, you must appreciate the appreciation of your clients as an important part of the reward for your work, but you must also keep an eye on cost efficiency. You must be technically competent and current, but you must pay equal attention to your communication skills. Your time will be flexible and often free, but you will be responsible for productive, workable, and accurate scheduling. And finally, you will be in a "helping" profession where competition has been increasing and will increase even further as larger firms, franchises, and entrepreneurial individuals join its ranks.

If you create a one-person firm, office politics will not be a factor in your career. Even in larger firms and franchise offices, there will be little formal supervision and no corporate ladders to climb. And you will probably join the vast majority of working home inspectors who applaud the freedom, the flexible hours, the varied workplaces, and the high degree of public contact.

Cheryll Brown, a home inspector in Minnesota and one of a handful of women in ASHI, believes that she has a particularly fine job for a woman with children because inspections can be scheduled when child care is available. She points out, however, that it's more difficult for a woman to establish credibility.

"It's got to do with the perception of women in our society," she says. "There seems to be a very elemental belief that women don't know much about home maintenance—*and shouldn't need to*!

"But it doesn't matter to me," she adds. "I believe that a woman can do everything in a home inspection that a man can do. And people will recognize this after a while. You just have to be aware that with each new client, you'll be required to prove yourself again."

Home inspection is a growth industry in an age of cutbacks. It is not without disadvantages, however. Income is not regular, there is rarely anyone around to substitute if you can't keep an appointment, and traditional company benefits just don't exist.

Many prospective home inspectors start out part-time to test the waters, as it were. Some augment their incomes by getting required local or state licenses for pest inspection, while others include radon testing in their service. And, of course, there is the temptation to offer to do (for a fee) the necessary repairs, a practice forbidden by Texas licensing laws and ASHI membership standards and discouraged by virtually every professional organization.

So what does it take? Honesty, motivation, perseverance, careful attention to detail, respect for others, good communication skills, some technical knowledge, some business knowledge, a relatively small amount of start-up cash, and the desire to be successful. If you're interested, there's room in the elevator. If you get in, you might go right to the top.

As a growing industry in a down economy, the career outlook for home inspectors is positive indeed. Each year over the last two decades, a larger percentage of home purchase contracts has been contingent on a professional inspection. In fact, the anxiety of consumers regarding the soundness of construction and the working order of major systems is so strong that government is now getting into the act also.

Six states—California, Kentucky, Maine, New Hampshire, Virginia, and Wisconsin—currently require home sellers to fill out a form disclosing defects. Twenty more states are likely to consider seller-disclosure bills within the next year. They are Alaska, Connecticut, Delaware, Hawaii, Illinois, Indiana, Louisiana, Maryland, Michigan, Mississippi, Missouri, Nebraska, New Mexico, New York, Ohio, Oklahoma, Oregon, Rhode Island, South Carolina, and Texas.

Twenty-six states, more than half the nation! Certainly this is a trend likely to continue. And with state governments encouraging wariness, certainly more and more home buyers will seek out the professional inspector.

## For More Information

Two national trade associations—the American Construction Inspectors Association and the American Society of Home Inspectors (ASHI)—have information available for the asking. Their addresses are listed in Appendix I.

The following are among the national franchises that will send you information on request:

Amerispec Home Inspection Service
1507 W. Yale Ave.
Orange, CA 92667
(800) 426-2270

The Building Inspector of America
684 Main St.
Wakefield, MA 01880
(800) 321-4677

HouseMaster of America, Inc.
421 W. Union Ave.
Bound Brook, NJ 08805
(800) 526-3939

National Property Inspections, Inc.
236 S. 108th Ave.
Omaha, NE 68154
(800) 333-9807

# It's Your Move

## *The Relocation Specialist*

What exactly is a relocation specialist, anyway? Are we talking about residential real estate salespeople? Do we include those appraisers who estimate value for the home to be sold or the home to be bought? And how about the sales reps (aka: moving consultants) for the moving van company? Or perhaps members of the corporate department that oversees transferring middle management personnel?

You don't know? Well, it's no wonder. The career is one of the new and growing opportunities of the 1990s, and its parameters are not yet firmly established. To some extent, it is a bit of all of the above, and yet it has become a specialty unto itself.

This is a career that grew out of a corporate need. The rapid growth of business in the late 1950s and early 1960s stimulated a policy of transferring employees to meet staffing needs for expansion. To entice top people to accept a move and to soothe their pain in being uprooted, relocation benefits were instituted and expanded in company after company. What started out as "We'll pay your moving expenses" gradually included help with the sale of a home, paid house-hunting trips, paid purchase closing costs, mortgage assistance if interest rates or cost of living differed between the old location and the new, spouse employment assistance, tax and legal advice, decorating expense allowances, and even counseling for children! Between 1973 and 1991, according to the Employee Relocation Council, the average cost to a corporation for relocating a home-owning employee went from $7,800 to $46,667.

"Wow!" you say. "But you still haven't told me exactly *what* a relocation specialist is."

Yes, it's time to set out the limits. The Employee Relocation Council (ERC) is the national professional association of organizations concerned with employee transfer. It lists among its members more than 1,200 representatives from corporations that relocate their employees and nearly 10,000 individuals and companies from the relocation industry, including real estate appraisers and brokers, area and personal counseling services, consulting services, home inspection companies, household goods movers, mortgage services, national house-buying firms, and a number of other relocation-related services. Each of these groups handles a specialized part of the relocation process, but for this chapter at least, we'll define relocation specialist as a professional who counsels and assists people in moving their households and who is paid a service fee not related to real estate commissions or moving costs.

Still not clear? Let's look at the responsibilities of the job.

## The Work

There is one point of general agreement: Being a relocation specialist is a service profession, providing help to people who are changing their place of residence. Career opportunities, however, exist in a number of business settings, some of which are focused on the move and some not. To begin to understand the career, you must understand how responsibilities and expectations vary, depending on who your employer is. Because there is tremendous overlap, we'll focus on the roles that are most essential to each of the following, and we'll look at differences between the employment venues.

### Within the Transferring Corporation

Employees with the title Relocation Specialist usually work in the human resources or personnel department (or whatever the department that handles employee services and problems is called). Usually, their primary responsibility is to advise employees about company policies regarding the move.

When independent relocation companies are not hired to see the transferee through the moving process, corporate relocation specialists also assist in choosing real estate agents in the new and old locations and supervise the paperwork involved in the relocation process on both ends. They also oversee the work of the third-party company, other property management consultants, the real estate agents, the mortgage brokers, the lawyers, and so on.

### In the Third-Party Company

Third-party companies manage the sale of the transferred employee's home. Sometimes, they actually buy the property; sometimes, they advance the equity to the homeowner but do not transfer title. In either case, the relocation specialist who works for a third-party company estimates fair market value, advises the home owner on the most effective marketing strategies, helps with legal and financial paperwork, and oversees the work of the real estate broker and the property management firm.

### In the Large Real Estate Broker's Office

Some larger firms now hire relocation specialists who work exclusively with transferees. These people do not, however, sell real estate. The relocation specialist introduces (and welcomes) the family to the area. He or she spends time getting to know their life-style, their likes and dislikes, their goals and hopes, and their financial resources and limitations.

Personalized area tours are designed and conducted to introduce the newcomers to the communities that will most likely meet their requirements. Videos, slides, or computer pictures of selected communities and even particular houses are sometimes shown in the office. Personalized welcome kits are prepared with extensive information on area services, recreation, schools, tax issues, future growth prospectives, and transportation and commuting questions.

Finally, the relocation specialist chooses a salesperson to help the family buy a home. Naturally, this agent is on the staff of the employing broker, but it is the relocation specialist's job to choose the agent most likely to be compatible with the personalities of the house-hunting family. When the family is choosing among two or more geographic areas that are widely separated (two suburbs, one east and one west of the city, for example), the relocation specialist will choose an agent in each of the two branch offices that best serve the areas concerned.

*In the Large, Specialized Relocation Company*

Corporations that transfer employees want their moves to be as smooth as possible. To minimize trauma, they often hire specialized relocation companies that are well staffed with relocation counselors. Some of these companies are independents, such as PHH Homequity, some are wholly owned subsidiaries of the largest brokers, such as Coldwell Banker Relocation, and some are affiliates of franchise organizations, such as Century 21's Western Relocation Management. No matter what the association of the relocation company, however, the relocation specialist is dedicated to protecting the interests of the client corporation and its transferees.

Work in the large relocation company has two sides: selling and buying. When advising sellers, the specialist not only suggests a probable selling price but also an asking price that will be effective for the pace of the local marketplace. He or she also suggests decorating and fix-up projects that may help to sell the property more quickly. A relocation specialist often works with the Realtor of choice on marketing strategies for the property. If the client moves before the property is sold, the relocation specialist may supervise the property management, the third-party company, and the real estate broker.

But the job goes beyond real estate. Relocation specialists at the initiation, (or home selling) end of the move also help to choose the best household goods mover and to solve special transportation problems, such as boats, extra vehicles, and even pets. Airline reservations, car rentals, hotels, even temporary housing and temporary furniture rental can also be a part of the service package. The specialist often also helps to choose destination housing areas and refers the transferees to Realtors in those areas.

On the destination end, advising arriving transferees includes all the responsibilities described above under "In the Large Real Estate Broker's Office" plus assistance in choosing the most suitable local brokers and sales agents and active participation in getting the best property at the best possible price. Some relocation consultants actually accompany the transferees and their Realtors on all house-hunting trips! Once a transferee chooses a potential property with a real estate agent, the relocation specialist is sometimes called in to do a competitive market analysis, using much the same methodology that an appraiser might use. Or the relocation specialist might order the CMA from the agent who is showing the property and then review it with the client for accuracy. The goal here is to assure the client that he or she is not overpaying for the property.

In the same vein of client protection, the relocation specialist will also check for local concerns. Is there a proposed highway that will pass nearby the property in question? Are zoning changes on the books? What's happening in the neighborhood schools? Is a tax revaluation imminent? And all those other questions that only someone following a local newspaper would have the answers to.

Finally, the relocation specialist will advise on financing sources, insurance, legal and closing assistance, and establishing local connections, such as banking and child care.

### In the Small Independent Relocation Company

The person who opens a relocation consulting firm with perhaps one or two assistants does everything the counselor in a large company does. These small firms sometimes specialize in a particular type of client, international or new hire, for example. Sometimes small independent firms also counsel people moving without corporate sponsorship, although public awareness of this service is just beginning to build. This can mean soup-to-nuts advice from the first thought of "How much can we get for this place?" to "Where and what should we buy? How do we do it?" Or it can mean a one-hour paid session in which the relocation specialist answers a list of questions posed by the home buyer/client.

As the owner of an independent firm, you will spend a good proportion of working time in canvassing area corporations, selling your services. This is competitive sales work similar in many ways to that done by mortgage brokers or home inspection firms, and the type of networking necessary for survival in those careers applies here.

As a job, relocation specialist can count variety among its appeal factors. The work is sometimes clerical and sometimes supervisory. There are many hours of personal interaction with clients, and there are many hours spent working alone gathering information and planning introductory tours. When the vacant homes of transferees must be managed, the job also takes on some aspects of the asset manager. Time is spent both in the office and on the road, some of it evenings and weekends. Dress is office professional, and a car is essential.

## The Money

If you define *client* as the one who pays for the service, the corporation doing the transferring, not the corporate transferee being counseled, is the client of the relocation specialist. Voicing an attitude that applies widely across the industry, Mike Robinson, president of Weichert Relocation in New Jersey, says, "Our goal is to provide the finest possible service to the transferee while actually saving money for the client corporation."

Fees charged the corporation are competitive and vary according to services provided and the going rates in the geographic area. In major metropolitan areas, a fee of $500 a day to provide a prospective employee or transferee an overview tour of the area is not uncommon.

Additional income for the relocation company is also earned through customary real estate commission splits. When a transferee buys a property through a broker recommended by the relocation specialist, it is common for the relocation firm to receive a referral fee (a percentage of the commission dollars earned by that selling broker). The amount of the referral commission is determined by mutual agreement, but 20 percent of the selling share is common.

For the individual relocation counselor working in a relocation company or a large real estate firm, income is usually an annual salary, often supplemented by a share of the referral commissions. Salaries vary from one company to another and in accordance with geographic area, but incomes in the $30,000 range are common for counselors. Administrators and managers of third-party holdings make more.

Because the relocation specialist is paid a fee that is not dependent on the buying or selling of property, advice to the transferee should be free of location prejudice or commission pressure. The goal of the work is unbiased counseling. Virtually all counselors agree that they are being paid at least in part for their objectivity.

## The People

It's generally recognized that moving is one of life's top ten stress situations. Assisting people through a move therefore must require highly developed interpersonal skills.

Gary Dittrich, president of Workforce Solutions in Stratford, Connecticut, has worked in the relocation industry since he left graduate school for a job with Homequity in 1977. Today, as head of a consulting firm to the relocation and banking industries, he believes that good listening skills are the key to satisfied relocation clients.

"I've heard the same story from so many transferees," Dittrich says. "They complain that the relocation company comes in and tells them how to solve all the problems of the move. But the transferees don't necessarily *want* those 'problems' solved. They have other concerns, and they feel short-changed because the relocation counselor doesn't deal with what they see as their particular problems. Most transferees wish their relocation counselor would listen more. If they listened carefully, then they would be able to understand the problems better and solve them more quickly."

As a destination specialist, Ellie Smith, president of Ellie Smith, Inc., in Basking Ridge, New Jersey, also advocates careful listening to get a clear perspective on each individual's and each family's needs. She and her staff develop a profile of each family member's lifestyle and then try to make a match with communities that will best meet their needs. "Each family is a puzzle," she says. "We just keep trying and moving the pieces until they all fit together."

Smith describes the range of interaction with different types of clients as marvelously wide. She has worked with college hires coming from life in a dormitory room or fraternity or sorority house. She has worked with international transferees who spoke little or no English and needed help in negotiating the aisles of the American supermarket. She has worked with top corporate executives who were introduced to real estate agents under a pseudonym to keep their positions from influencing their property negotiations. And she has worked with "typical" American families. "It's all part of what makes this a wonderful job!" she declares.

Petie Prybylski, who works with Smith, adds that as wonderful as it may be, it's also very complex. Whether initiating the move or helping the newly arrived transferee to settle in, the relocation specialist rarely deals with one person only. There always seems to be "family" involved in some way or another, and dealing with the interrelationships and the varying needs of each person is an important part of the work.

Mary Anne Hashem of Prudential Network Realty says, "Transferees are older now than they were years ago. We're often working with people in their 40s and 50s. Where once we spent a lot of time focused on small children, now we have teenage or adult children and sometimes parents to consider. Sometimes we even need as many as *three* homes or apartments. A transferee will say, for example, 'We're bringing my mother and mother-in-law with us,' and we begin three different searches."

Whenever there's a network of people involved in a move, there are also career questions and problems beyond those of the transferee. There's the career of the spouse to consider and sometimes even the careers of adult children. When the question of commuting patterns comes up, for example, the relocation specialist may have to deal with it on several levels. The same applies to recreation, shopping, medical care, education, and community services.

It's not easy. Moving at the end of the millennium has become an event with strings attached. "It all adds to the trauma of the move for these people," sums up Hashem. "So they don't just walk up to a home and say, 'I love it!'"

In addition to working *with* transferees and their families, the relocation specialist works *for* them. In the role of representative or advocate, he or she must deal with countless people in varying positions of authority. The list includes lawyers, bankers, Realtors, movers, the clerks who guard the deposit monies for local utilities, car rental agents, furniture rental suppliers, travel agents . . . well, you get the idea!

Inevitably, there are problems. Things can go wrong, and they do. Then it often falls to the relocation specialist to be mediator and sometimes mentor. Do we need to say that patience, perseverance, and well-developed interpersonal skills are essential to the job?

Finally, "working with people" includes those in the office. The relocation specialist must work with the supervisors and the support staff in his or her company. There are always forms to fill out and meetings to attend. In larger firms, there may be weekly or monthly evaluation sessions, either in groups or one-on-one with a supervisor. There's absolutely no question that the successful person in this career must be able to take advice as well as give it.

## Getting In

Where do relocation specialists come from? You might be surprised.

Betty Votta, a vice-president of Weichert Relocation, holds a master's degree in English literature and taught for many years in both high school and college before starting her present career. Who's on her hiring list now? "They must have a real estate salesperson's license," she replies.

That criterion doesn't apply universally, however. Louise Zabel, an associate of Ellie Smith, was originally a dietitian. Sandra Peterson of Dallas, Texas, started in accounting. Donna Harbour of Troy, Michigan, was an account executive for an audiovisual firm. Gary Dittrich majored in political science. The list could go on and on.

Although real estate sales really is the most common forerunner to the career of relocation specialist, other previous careers that appeal to the top executives who do the hiring are teaching and nursing. One top broker in Texas also liked to hire former waiters and waitresses because they had learned patience with difficult people. In a word, the career appeals to people with a disposition to helping. Besides the service perspective, many relocation companies look for problem-solving skills.

But you don't need special degrees or certificates to enter this profession. As long as you do not act as an agent in the sale and purchase of real estate, there is no licensing requirement for the job. At the end of the 1980s, the Employee Relocation Council did introduce two professional designations: Certified Relocation Professional (CRP) and Senior Certified Relocation Professional (SCRP). Both require membership in the organization, experience in the field, and passing scores on specialized examinations. These professional credentials, however, are not required for success or promotion in the field.

## Is This for You?

If you know the nuts and bolts of the real estate business, if you hate sales but enjoy service, and if you really know your local geographic area, relocation may be your cup of tea. The job requires a detail-oriented person who can also be outgoing. Most of all, it requires the ability to listen and to interpret what you hear in the light of the moving situation.

If you like new faces, the career of relocation specialist has the advantage of new customers virtually every week. You will be dealing with these people on a highly personal level as they seek new homes in a new community or deal with the pain of uprooting. Some of them will become your friends because you will work with them in a support role without the pressure of sales. Sometimes at the end of a day's work or after a difficult transferee has been placed, you'll simply feel good. You've helped someone through a problem. On the other hand, sometimes you'll be ready to pull your hair out when things just can't get resolved.

If you wish to be promoted in a large relocation company or want to open your own firm, you'll have to move some of your time out of work with transferred families and into the sales arena, soliciting the business of corporations that move people or selling the firm's services to banks who want their foreclosed properties managed. This change takes the relocation specialist out of the helping mode and into sales and may not appeal to everyone.

The future of the relocation business looks promising as more and more companies outsource (hire outside contractors for) their relocation work and as the buying and selling of property becomes still more specialized and complex. Gary Dittrich sees excellent training programs being developed on the technical and processing side of the relocation business, thus creating many opportunities for people from very different backgrounds.

"There is a need in the industry, however, for good problem solvers," he says. "But I mean *creative* problem solvers, people who can look at a situation from many perspectives and come up with original solutions."

## For More Information

The Employee Relocation Council is the trade organization for the profession. They have material on their membership available. See Appendix I for the address.

*National Relocation and Real Estate* is a trade magazine. Each issue contains a listing called "Relocation Service Company Profiles," which includes addresses, telephone numbers, and the names of principals, as well as areas of service and specialties. This information can be invaluable in a job search. Single copies are available for $5.95; the subscription rate is $41.65 per year. An annual directory of the relocation business is also available for $95. For more information, write to Relocation Information Service, Inc., at 113 Post Rd. E, Westport, CT 06880, or phone (203) 227-3800.

# Teaching, Lecturing, and Training in Real Estate

You know a lot in your specialty and would like to share that knowledge, helping others on their path to the success you now enjoy. Teaching, you feel, will reward that altruistic side of your nature.

It will also bring in a little extra money. Emphasis is on the "little" in the more common teaching situations, because we are talking about the field of education, which, in the main, is not as financially rewarding as many realty careers. Of course, there are far more real estate professionals teaching, training, and lecturing as a sideline than those who are engaged full time as professors.

Money aside, there *is* a satisfaction that comes from helping others and perhaps just the tiniest delight, too, in being attached to a college or university, telling the young, or not-so-young, about your success, how you spend your days, what you think of your particular field, and how you would change a few things here and there. Oh, and naturally, you will be teaching the course too. That you want to talk about your world a couple of hours a week is understandable. Teaching may enhance your real estate career as well, offering opportunities for new connections. It also looks good on a résumé.

All of the opportunities that exist for teaching real estate cannot be discussed in detail in these few pages. For example, you can conduct your own seminars, or you can become an instructor in someone else's all-day workshops, perhaps traveling around the country. You must really know your field, of course, and if you run seminars on your own, you must understand that this is a serious, many-faceted business. You will be responsible for staff, marketing, transportation, hiring facilities at each location, and so on.

If you want to teach advanced courses in your own specialty

to those in your field, you might consider local lectures or workshops for your national professional association. Most of those
organizations conduct periodic brush-up courses or new ones for
their members at different locations around the country. At the
simplest level, you can even teach a few local folks interested in
your subject at your own dining table.

Those with practically an encyclopedic knowledge of the buy/
sell/invest field might want to approach a local radio station and
suggest doing a call-in program to answer listeners' questions
each week.

The next few pages look at the most likely teaching posts for
those already engaged in some area of the huge real estate arena.
From these descriptions you should be able to decide whether
becoming Ms. or Mr. Chips is a part-time or full-time career you
might enjoy and whether you would do well as a member of an
academic community.

## The Work

For those with no particular academic credentials—that can
include no college degree or no postgraduate credentials—there
are almost always teaching opportunities at evening adult schools
sponsored by local four-year, junior, or community colleges or
held under the aegis of county or municipal offices.

You can teach anything you like as long as the administration
feels you can bring in enough students to "make," as they say in
this field, a class. Six or ten students might be the minimum.
Your credentials are not a PhD, but rather your years of experience in your field and how you present yourself to the administration.

You probably would not be able to make a class in property
management at Elm St. High School's Adult Education Series,
but one on how to buy a home or how to make money buying and
rehabbing houses might go over very well.

You might like to take on a little more than adult ed, perhaps
teaching credit college courses. With the growing number of
colleges and universities offering undergraduate and graduate
real estate programs, it is possible that you could find a niche for
yourself in the halls of academe.

At the college or university level, you might want to become an
adjunct professor (some of the top-flight schools do not have

adjuncts, however). These are part-time instructors, and in some institutions today, they outnumber full-time teachers by two or even three to one, although in the view of the American Association of University Professors, no more than 15 percent of campus instruction should be assigned to part-time teachers. Many community colleges, however, faced with continuing budget cuts and the mandate to open their doors to all high school graduates, have been hiring more and more adjuncts over the last several years. On the other hand, another, smaller group of schools has cut back on adjuncts because of protests from students (and their parents) and because the teaching formerly done by adjuncts is now being handled by graduate assistants, who spend more time on campus.

Adjuncts have no office at the school, so if you choose this route to the classroom, you will have to forego visions of yourself settled in some comfortable, if small, office, books all around you, feeling quite professorial. There is no heady dose of "college atmosphere" for adjuncts, which might be translated into sitting around and chatting with other faculty members. Adjuncts are often required to give students their home telephone numbers, and that is how they are available after hours to their class. Adjuncts can teach in the daytime, or they can teach evening classes, perhaps in a school's extension program for those working toward a degree after work hours.

Theoretically, adjuncts are supposed to possess the same academic credentials as full-time instructors, which means a doctorate or at least a master's degree, but that rule is waived more than applied, and many of those who do have the requisite initials after their names have specialties in fields tangential to the subject they are hired to teach. Other qualifications are at the discretion of the school. One faculty union president of a community college is on record as saying, "We have certainly accepted as adjuncts people who we would never have hired full time." At some community colleges, life experience (that is, real estate experience) can substitute for a master's degree, but you will almost certainly have to possess an undergraduate degree, although again, any major will usually be acceptable.

Four-year colleges and some junior colleges require a doctorate, or terminal degree, to teach as a tenured member of the faculty. This degree requirement is a stumbling block for many experienced real estate professionals who want to quit the town for the gown. No exceptions are made here, and, of course, there are not many top-flight developers, star real estate salespeople, or owners of a dozen or so shopping centers who hold doctorates of any type.

"You've got to have your card punched," says Dr. Dennis S. Tosh, of the real estate department at the University of Mississippi. "That means you need a PhD. People who don't have one will get a job at a junior college or community college, many of which are reasonably lenient. But a school that is fully accredited at the national level will require that degree." Tosh added that Ole Miss does not use any part-timers in teaching real estate.

The degree requirement can frustrate teachers too. "There are a lot of people out there I know have the knowledge to teach a particular skill-type class," says Beverly McCormick, "but because of their degree, or, more correctly, lack thereof, we can't hire them." McCormick is chair of real estate studies at Morehead State University, in Morehead, Kentucky. She adds that a small regional school has a particularly difficult time attracting those with the needed credentials to teach real estate. "Here in eastern Kentucky, that's really a problem," she says. McCormick teaches a number of real estate courses at the school and has a background as a practicing lawyer (her terminal degree of LLD allows her to teach).

McCormick was attending law school while her husband, who is also an attorney, was in practice. "I noticed that most of real estate is law," she recalls. She entered private practice for a few years after graduating and then headed for teaching. "I love it," she says. "I just really love teaching."

McCormick's background in law brings up an interesting point: Many of those teaching credit real estate courses these days are lawyers, partly because so much of real estate is indeed related to the law, but also because lawyers are the only real estate professionals who have that necessary doctorate.

Leaving the adjunct level and becoming a full-timer on a college faculty, you might start at the instructor level, which is not a tenure-track position on many campuses and calls for only a master's degree. The doctorate, remember, is needed for tenure. With that degree you will likely enter at the assistant professor level, moving to associate professor, and finally to full professor. At some colleges, you can pursue your doctorate at that institution while teaching, at no cost to you. You will then be simultaneously a teacher and a student.

Incidentally, while some colleges offer a real estate major, in many others there might be just one or two specific real estate courses taught under the umbrella of the business or finance department.

As far as the work itself is concerned, Tosh explained that being on the faculty at many large four-year schools takes in three elements. First there is the teaching itself. Next is research. "They are always going to be expected to do a fair amount of research in real estate until they are tenured," Tosh points out. The third element rounding out the teacher's responsibilities is service. In many instances, real estate programs are funded by real estate commissions or professional associations in that region, and for their investment, those organizations request the staff in a real estate department to conduct research for them and work on other realty-related projects. The amount of work can vary from the occasional request to a great volume of studies, projects, and so on.

There is another opportunity for those who are interested in teaching, although in this case *training* might be the better term. All national real estate franchises and large regional, privately owned agencies have in-house training programs that use instructors taken from the employee pool or hired from the outside.

Coldwell Banker might be typical. Its in-house program trains newcomers, updates seasoned professionals, and instructs everyone on new projects and programs. The Coldwell Banker University, which is just a few years old, offers two core curricula: the Sales Institute and the Management Institute. The former provides progressive training for sales associates and includes courses in personal business development, win-win negotiations, sales communication, listing strategies for a competitive market, and proactive listing. Among the courses in the Management Institute are Financial Management, Coaching Clinic, Situational Leadership, and Avoidance of Legal Problems. Each institute is offered in three progressive levels of required and elective courses, and upon completion, a diploma is awarded to the "graduate."

Coldwell Banker University is directed by Robert Quick, vice-president of international training. The first dean of CBU is

Joseph P. Klock, a real estate author, lecturer, trainer, and residential specialist. An affable dean ("call me Joe"), Klock notes that Coldwell Banker uses both employee instructors and outside contract teachers. In-house employees can ask to be trainers if they think they have the right stuff (described later), or they can be tapped on the shoulder and invited to join that force.

"We have about 2,000 locations and about 50,000 people who need to be trained and retrained on a continuing basis," says Klock, "and some are in offbeat locations too. Some trainers work inside, and some are on the road all the time. There is a constant need here because even if you are in some small town in Pennsylvania doing a program, tomorrow or the day after tomorrow there will be someone new there who will need training."

Training consists of lecturing and classroom participation, of course, but Klock says Coldwell Banker hopes "to be using video, interactive video, and perhaps teleconferencing" in its programs eventually, "getting more and more high tech."

Klock does a little instructing in the field, but he lives 3,000 miles from Coldwell Banker's home office in Mission Viejo, California, so his is not a 9-to-5 workday. He is an employee of Coldwell Banker, however.

## The Money

Teaching adult, or continuing, education pays about $20 to $30 an hour, usually for two hours once a week for six weeks.

Adjunct professors receive about $1,200 to teach one three-credit course two or three times a week for a total of about three hours a week per semester. That pay is about 40 percent of what it costs in salary and benefits for a full-time teacher to conduct the same course.

Above the adjunct level at four-year colleges, junior colleges, and community colleges, there is a broad range of pay scales. Telling you that salaries can range from $15,000 a year to more than $60,000 is probably going to be of little help to you in determining your own likely paycheck. Income depends on the teacher's credentials, the amount of teaching, research, and publishing done by him or her, and the size, reputation, and location of the school. Obviously, the high-end figure doesn't seem to be bad at all when one considers that this is a field generally considered poor paying. Remember, though, that the academic credentials required and the sum of money spent acquiring degrees and knowledge might well translate into higher earnings in the private sector. Also, those pulling in top salaries on the campus are likely to be the few top "stars," heads of department, or both.

Trainers working for real estate companies are salaried, except for contract people who are paid on a per diem basis. Salaries vary from one firm to another, but overall, trainers can expect to earn between $20,000 and $50,000 a year. Those at the top of the pyramid earn substantially more. Professionals who head national training programs, for example, have incomes of $125,000 to $150,000 a year.

## The People

When you teach either continuing ed or for-credit college courses, you will find that there are two segments you will have to interact with: your students and the other members of the faculty, especially the chair of your department. There is not as much supervision in adult education, but as an adjunct you will be reviewed. A professor from your department will sit in on one of your classes during your first year and will rate your performance, an assessment that is added to your personnel file. If you are on a tenure track, you will be reviewed annually and will pretty much "audition" for about six years until tenure is yours. (The beauty of tenure, of course, is that once you possess it, you cannot be fired from that institution unless you burn down the administration building.)

Although you will be in an academic atmosphere that might be quite enjoyable on some level and certainly very different from the corporate world or on-site work, you will likely find the professional camaraderie you seek easier as a full-time professor than as an adjunct (remember, adjuncts do not even have a desk and chair on campus).

However, enjoyment of the student-teacher relationship in the classroom and satisfaction from watching your teaching and ideas take hold can, of course, be found during day classes or at evening school for those who hold the loftiest or the lowliest titles.

When you begin teaching, will you feel a part of the college community, or will you continue to belong more to the world of real estate? Tosh, whose background is in appraising and whose specialty ("You need a specialty, too," he says) is appraising compliance for financial institutions, laughs at the question.

"That depends on what time of the day it is and what day of the week," he replies. On a more serious note, he adds, "Until you're tenured, you have to be doing so much research you don't have time to ally yourself with anything but the computer or the library."

## Getting In

To enter the field of continuing education, you will probably approach a school with your interest in teaching, but sometimes your high profile in the community or in your area of expertise brings the college to you. David T. Schumacher, whom you met in Chapter 2 on buying and rehabbing houses, also taught off and on during his varied real estate career, and his first experience was by invitation.

Schumacher's background is in appraising, which he practiced while acquiring a substantial real estate portfolio in the Hermosa Beach area of Southern California. "I used to be director of training and research for one of the largest appraising companies in the country," he recalled, "and one day someone from a local night school called me and asked me to teach a class in appraising. 'When?' I asked. She said, 'Tonight.' I said, 'I'll be right over.' So I did it for five years."

If no one is knocking on your door, write the administrator of the continuing education department at the college that interests you or any other sponsor of adult education where you live. Besides mentioning your credentials, tell them briefly what you would cover in the class—no formal syllabus is required here—and why you think some folks in your community would be interested in signing up to learn. Be sure your letter is virtually perfect because it is your marketing tool. You will want to address the administrator by name, of course. The fall semester starts in September, the winter term in January, and summer school in June. Contact the appropriate person several months in advance of the term you prefer.

If you get the green light to teach, send out a press release to local papers, including the weekly freebies, announcing the availability of the course, where it will be held, who is sponsoring it, what it will cost, and a little (no more than one or two sentences) about your credentials. Direct your release to the community news department or any other section of the paper likely to publish that brief notice. The school will send out a course catalog, but your promoting the availability of your own course might just help you sign up the required number of students to allow you to teach.

We have already described the requirements for getting in at the adjunct, instructor, assistant, associate, and full professor levels at colleges and universities. Here, too, you might be invited to teach, or you might have to approach the real estate or business department head with your letter and credentials. You should know that the search for someone to fill a specific teaching slot usually starts a year before that individual is expected to begin teaching, so it is unlikely that you can decide in May that you want to become Professor Smith in September and then go right out and find a position. Hiring practices can be very drawn out.

What sort of professionals make good trainers for real estate companies? Joseph Klock considers some traits to be particularly important. "Obviously, we are talking about presentation skills," he explains.

That is the most important. Knowledge in the field is helpful, but not absolutely necessary. We train you. Of course, the chances of someone with no experience at all becoming a trainer are pretty slim because there are so many people who have it.

I look for people who have the burn, the desire, to train. That can override even the presentation skills. You know, I've seen two types of people. The first type learns something, and his automatic instinct is to grab hold and run home and do it. The other person can't wait to go home and teach someone else to do it. The first type is in sales; the second is a trainer. These are people who could make a hell of a lot of money doing something else, but they love to teach.

The difference between us and college professors is that with the professors, once they impart knowledge, their job is done. In our business, after people learn and *actually do it*, then our job is done.

## Is This for You?

By now you should have a very good idea about whether teaching is for you and whether you will be accepted at the institution of your choice.

Besides knowledge of your subject, teaching skills are required, of course, at the college and even the adult-ed level. The latter courses call for some preparation and, like any teaching, require the instructor to listen as well as talk, provide a forum for discussion in the classroom, and possess other skills. If you know absolutely nothing about the techniques of teaching, you might contact the Real Estate Educators Association (REEA), which comprises college teachers, corporate lecturers, proprietary school teachers, writers, and others interested in real estate education. They can help you with course materials.

On the college level, we have already discussed what is required, from advanced degrees to the willingness to put in time doing research in the field. If you are going to retain your principal job and teach part time, at whatever level, you must be able to switch hats quickly from the corporate to the academic world, two very different sciences. Neither job can be short-changed, of course.

If becoming a trainer at a real estate company interests you, you will, as Klock put it, need "the burn" far more than for instructing students at a college or university. You cannot just teach and walk away—and maybe the students will learn the material and maybe they won't. In the real estate company, you lecture and then must wait and see that your students put to use the curriculum you have just taught. Only then is your work completed.

Do any of these teaching or training slots sound like you? Then by all means, no matter how different those worlds seem from what you are doing now, look into the possibility of taking on new responsibilities in that new arena. Besides the good feeling that comes from helping others to learn and the extra money if you decide you want to teach part time, for those who have been engaged in one aspect or another of real estate, teaching can open new windows of opportunity, bringing fresh challenges, satisfying work, and, for some, perhaps an entirely new career.

Schumacher, who taught at the University of California's extension program for 16 years, along with his stint in continuing ed, notes: "I taught people who didn't have to come to school. They were also out in the field. Some of the most exciting experiences I had were when those people challenged me on what I said. I like to have people tell me where I made a mistake or how things in general can be corrected. That was the greatest experience of my life."

## For More Information

*How to Teach Real Estate to Adults*, by Donald R. Levi, is available from the Real Estate Educators Association. It covers classroom arrangement, using equipment, stimulating discussion among students, clothing and body language, and preparing tests, among other topics. At this writing, the book costs $14.95, but the association suggests you check with them for the current price before placing an order. (See Appendix I for the address.)

# PART II | Another 15 Opportunities

# Residential Property Management

There always seems to be a "Help Wanted" sign out for residential property managers. Those who find this specialty of interest should see this as encouraging. Look around your town, and you will get some idea of the phenomenal growth in management opportunities during, say, the last decade. Rental apartment complexes, cooperative and condominium communities, home owner associations, mobile home parks, and some single-family houses are overseen by property managers.

This chapter considers managers who are engaged by building owners or who work for full-service property management companies. Professionals who serve as asset managers, hired by lending institutions, insurance companies, and government agencies, are covered in Chapter 12, which discusses careers in that arena, which is less hands-on than the responsibilities we will explore in the next several pages.

The role of the property manager is to handle day-to-day operations of an investment that is not simply a file folder of papers. The work includes hiring service people; paying bills; assigning maintenance, repair, and renovation jobs; overseeing security procedures; and handling staffing, advertising, accounting, and taxes. The property manager must also visit the site frequently, talk with tenants or home owners, and listen to their concerns and complaints. The manager or management firm might also lease rental units, although sometimes there is a separate individual or staff for that purpose.

Apartment building owners typically pay the management firm a percentage of the rent roll for their services. Condominium associations might pay a flat fee or any other agreed-on charge.

Property management is a salaried, not commissions-only,

profession. A real estate license is usually not required unless a company requests it of its managers.

If the number of residential units likely to need professional management has grown over the last decade or so, the profession of management has leaped forward even more. "It used to be more of a mom-and-pop operation," says Connie Patterson. "You had the woman who collected rents and her husband who handled the maintenance work, and they lived on premises." Patterson is vice-president of operations for the property management division of Shannon & Luchs, a major firm in the Washington, D.C., area. Besides property management, the firm comprises insurance, commercial brokerage, and residential sales divisions.

Patterson's background recalls what now seems like "the old days" in property management, although those times are as recent as the mid-1970s. She graduated from college with a degree in education and taught school for four years before moving to Washington, D.C. It was difficult for her to secure another teaching position in her new hometown, but another opportunity presented itself, making hers a typical "this was my convoluted path into real estate" story.

While Patterson was still fairly new to her apartment house in the district, she saw an opening for a desk clerk there. Well, why not? She was, after all, unemployed. She filled in at that post while continuing her "serious" search for a teaching position. This was a brand-new apartment building, with units open only through the second floor. The owners were staffing the property at the time and had a number of positions to fill. They asked Patterson, who was apparently making an excellent desk clerk pro tem, if she would like to rent apartments. "I said, 'I'll try it,'" she recalls. "Then they asked me, 'Would you like to be assistant manager?' I said 'I'll try it.'"

And thus was born another real estate career. Patterson stayed with that company—which developed, built, and managed its own properties—for 12 years, leaving to become a vice-president at Shannon & Luchs, which had a larger portfolio of properties. Indeed, Shannon & Luchs manages more than 6,000 residential units, 6.4 million square feet of commercial space, and some retail footage.

Over the last several years, more and more emphasis has been placed on what is going on in the home, or headquarters, office of a management firm over apartment communities "in the field."

Although on-site property managers still exist, that is now seen almost as a career in itself. There is more about the position of on-site manager later in this chapter.

In the corporate world, the changes have been significant. The path to a senior executive position in a management firm once often began with living in a small apartment complex and running that community for the firm. These days, although there is always opportunity for talented and determined individuals, broadly speaking, resident manager positions no longer automatically lead up the corporate ladder.

Patterson notes, "I know a lot of my contemporaries started as on-site managers or marketing managers or assistant managers. Then over time and a lot of hard work we were able to elevate ourselves. But over maybe the last two or three years, there have been incredible changes in property management, more changes than over the 15 years prior to that."

There has been much pressure in the business from building owners who need strong financial assistance, not only in managing their properties, but also in anticipating problems in other areas of their portfolios. As a result, today's property manager must be very astute financially.

These days, the profession calls for managers with a broader perspective than a focus on just one property. Managers must be able to look at a residential complex, for example, and ask—and be able to answer—"Will this property bring more than $600 a month for each unit, given its somewhat problem location? Does it make sense to make a lot of improvements to this property?" Professionals must be able to anticipate every eventuality for their properties. Building owners hold managers accountable for many of their problems. Not only will owners complain of competition, for instance, but they will also expect managers to have spotted the competitors and have a solid plan for doing battle with them. "Why didn't you tell me there's a new building going up near my Highrise Towers?" demands today's landlord. "My tenants are telling me those people are offering them lower rents, and they're leaving. What do I do now?" The property manager had better have an answer.

"Owners are now looking at their properties and seeing this is a business," says Patterson, "not just an investment they have waiting in the wings for their grandchildren."

Who are the successful candidates for property management

careers? College graduates with degrees in business, finance, marketing, or management are welcome at the large property management firms because they presumably have the ability to work on a variety of management problems and challenges. Those who have taken specific courses in property management in college receive an even brighter greeting at personnel offices.

Every property management firm has its own career progression, of course, but they are essentially similar to the career path at Shannon & Luchs. A beginner there enters as an administrative assistant, working closely with an established property manager. He or she sees how the company functions internally, goes out occasionally with the manager to visit a community, and in general spends about 18 months learning the nuts and bolts of the business.

The employee then moves up to become an assistant property manager. He or she continues to work closely with an experienced professional but is now given a little more responsibility, helps solve some problems, and grows beyond the entry-level stage.

Gradually, the intense supervision disappears, the number or quality of properties in the assistant's portfolio increases, the title changes, and he or she is on the road to the few slots at the top of the corporate pyramid.

Who would *not* do well in this field? Patterson responds, "Someone who has trouble with numbers or handling a multitude of things simultaneously. You have 689 balls in the air at the same time here. Some people have difficulty organizing their priorities."

Patterson's own responsibilities include hiring property managers, meeting with her managers weekly, meeting with senior property managers every other week, and making an annual on-site inspection, with the owner and property manager, of every building or complex under the Shannon & Luchs management umbrella. "I try to do it around budget time," she explains. "Owners need to see what's what with their properties. They'll agree to more of our recommendations in the budget if they see firsthand what we're trying to do"

Woven throughout this career choice, from the beginning level to senior staff positions, is the presence of the Institute of Real Estate Management (IREM), a professional association that offers career guidance and certification. IREM is an affiliate of the

National Association of Realtors. All serious beginners in property management take IREM courses (Patterson teaches one for on-site managers). IREM certification—several programs are offered—is eventually expected by building owners and management concerns.

Brenda Austin holds an Accredited Residential Manager (ARM) certification in her position as on-site manager of a 100-unit rental complex in Arkansas. Her staff includes an assistant manager, a maintenance person, a groundskeeper, and other service people who are called in as needed (carpet cleaning, maid services, and the like).

On-site managers are, of course, given an apartment on premises, which is calculated into their salary. Salaries depend on many factors, including the area of the country, the size and luxury level of the apartment complex, and the policy of the owner or management firm doing the hiring. The more difficult, or troubled, properties command a higher salary. Government-subsidized or government-assisted communities also require more work, for which the manager expects a higher paycheck. The latter buildings and complexes call for income and other screenings of prospective tenants, periodic reexamination of tenants regarding eligibility, and other duties not called for in open-market rental properties.

The career progression in this field is to larger, more prestigious property. Interestingly, although corporate property management positions are not held overwhelmingly by men or women, at the on-site level almost 80 percent of managers are women. Professionals in the field say that it could be because some women enjoy the interaction that the position calls for, preferring it over the less people-oriented corporate world. Job requirements are not as stiff for on-site managers as they are for trainees at management firms.

Austin's background includes several years spent with a major motel chain, working her way up from desk clerk to assistant general manager. She is used to working with people and says that this is the principal quality needed in an on-site manager. "Every day is a challenge," she notes, "because you are dealing with all different types of people. You *must* be a people person to do well in this job. You have to allow tenants to vent their feelings without reacting yourself, which means having a lot of self-control. You have to keep both residents and the owner happy at the same time." Austin is employed by the owner of her complex, not a management company. She must be doing a commendable job of keeping everyone happy. She has won several IREM awards for on-site management.

Patterson, who hires on-site managers for Shannon & Luchs, echoes Austin's statement. "People skills are number one because you are dealing with families and homes," she explains.

> Supervising a staff also calls for talent in dealing with people. I also look for applicants who can speak well and write well. That doesn't mean a Harvard MBA, just a basic understanding of communicating—and of numbers because you need to understand budgets.

> But it all goes back to getting along with people. We manage a number of senior citizen residences, and we look for certain skills in our managers there. I've found that individuals who are not people-oriented will find these jobs wear them down very quickly. They just do not have the psychological energy to stay with the day-to-day work and challenges.

Those who do have what it takes can enjoy a fine career in on-site management and might perhaps, but not assuredly, move into higher management. Those who bring savvy 1990s marketing and financing skills to the field will find a different and broader opportunity, at the home office level, in this always-growing specialty.

## For More Information

*Property Management*, by Robert C. Kyle and Floyd M. Baird (Chicago: Dearborn Financial Publishing, 1991), $39.95, offers a comprehensive look at this career choice. It includes sample forms, quizzes, a helpful glossary of terms, and some creative ideas for property managers. The book also looks at shopping center management. If you can't find it in bookstores, write to the publisher at 520 N. Dearborn St., Chicago, IL 60610. Add sales tax where applicable, plus $5.00 for shipping.

The Institute of Real Estate Management offers an annual catalog of publications (including textbooks), courses, and programs. Their address can be found in Appendix I.

# Asset Management

If you hear the word *portfolio* and think of a group of properties to be managed rather than an oversized folder containing an artist's drawings, you may belong in this executive branch of the property management industry. The professional real estate asset manager oversees the management of an entire portfolio of investment properties. He or she may head the property management department of a large corporation, work in a large specialized property management firm, or head a small independent property management firm.

Asset management opportunities are now growing because the current trend in business is toward outsourcing some of the functions that are tangential to the primary work of the corporation. Property management is among those corporate concerns that are being subcontracted to smaller specialized companies. For example, hot on the list of job opportunities in the mid-1990s is asset management for lending institutions. Some banks are hiring specialists to manage their portfolios; others are hiring relocation, real estate, and/or property management firms to provide asset managers who will take the responsibility for efficient and profitable, or at least money-saving, management. Let's take a closer look at the work in the lending community.

Do you know about nonperforming assets? Can you list the steps in the foreclosure process in your state? Have you heard the acronym *REO*? If you answered yes to all these questions, you may be on your way to providing asset management service to a lending institution.

For the past several decades in the overlapping worlds of real estate and banking, the term *asset management* has pretty much referred to work centered around the disposition (that is, the sale, by whatever means available) of foreclosed properties. These properties are known in the business as real estate owned, or REOs.

Even in the best of times, most banks have had some REOs on

the books, more during economic downturns. Always, someone was in charge of getting rid of these nonperforming assets. As long as that person did the job with reasonable expediency, no one paid much attention. Then we hit the end of the 1980s.

Across the nation, property foreclosures spread like chicken pox. Many banks that might have been carrying a dozen REOs in 1985 found themselves carrying hundreds at the turn of the decade. Suddenly, the very survival of a lending institution often depended on the effective management of its REOs. The career of asset manager then took on a new profile.

Banks actively sought out men and women with bulging portfolios of "workouts" that had been successfully managed. The term *workout* refers to a process that starts with putting foreclosure pressure on a nonperforming loan, moves to restructuring the loan or to repossession, and finally goes on to disposition of the property. Joseph B. Tockarshewsky was such a man.

When he was named president and CEO of Poughkeepsie Savings in July 1992, the bank had posted 13 consecutive money-losing quarters, and its inventory of nonperforming assets totaled $105 million. Soon after he took the helm, he hired five more executives who were experienced in asset management. In January 1993, the bank reported a profit of $3.1 million for the fourth quarter of 1992.

To fill the role of asset manager, Tockarshewsky stresses the need for both a thorough understanding of the real estate marketplace and an open and creative mind. "Every deal is unique," he says.

> You have to evaluate all aspects of the situation and understand it intimately before you do anything. Then you begin to make decisions. Foreclosure is not always the right answer. Sometimes it's best to advise and support the borrower or to bring in some new investors. When foreclosure is necessary, the asset manager must work to get clear title as quickly as possible and then proceed to an effective marketing plan in order to sell the property.
>
> In the end, it boils down to time and money. Price is always the most important factor in a sale, but establishing price is an art in these multimillion-dollar deals. Do you put money into the project to make it more attractive? Or do you price low to move the property quickly? It's always a

balancing act. The good asset manager can keep all factors in mind while remaining open to creative solutions. Then in the final analysis, he or she moves to bring the best return in the least amount of time.

Not all banks have the bulk of their nonperforming assets in multimillion-dollar projects, as Poughkeepsie Savings did. Many are holding huge inventories of one- to four-family houses. These lenders often hire people with real estate experience to manage their portfolios.

With a background in real estate sales and experience with a third-party relocation company, Preston Maynard was named manager of residential REOs at People's Bank in Bridgeport, Connecticut, in the summer of 1992. In his position, he oversees the foreclosure process, arranges for time- and market-conscious estimates of property value, hires, supervises, and evaluates local real estate brokers to handle the marketing and sale of each individual property, arranges for refurbishing if it is cost-effective, and supervises the supplementary bank advertising in local newspapers.

"You don't have to cut prices and run," says Maynard. "You can market aggressively and maintain value. Our goal is moving property, not dumping it, and our average sale price is at 93 percent of appraised value."

Although overwhelmed by the sheer numbers of their REOs, some lenders are unwilling to change the bank management to a real estate orientation or even to expand the asset management department to include real estate sales specialists. Instead, they are outsourcing. In doing so, they are stimulating the growth of an industry.

Since the 1970s, relocation firms like PHH Homequity have advised sellers about property value and marketability and then managed the sale. These firms are now developing specialized departments or wholly owned subsidiaries to work with lenders that have large REO inventories. Weichert Relocation, a subsidiary of Weichert Realtors, which is one of the nation's largest brokerage firms, recently named Frank Palestrini vice-president— inventory management to oversee the management of large bank portfolios of residential properties.

Palestrini points out the advantages of centralized management of a diverse and geographically scattered portfolio. "Our focus is intense and specialized," he says. "Anyone needing information on any bank property can get it immediately from us. We have knowledge and control of all the available resources, and we always make decisions with our first responsibility to the owner of the REOs."

Another new firm, Metland Properties Group, located in New Jersey, specializes in handling failed multiunit development projects for lenders. With a background in both real estate sales and property development, John G. Udell, president of Metland, says his firm is one of the few in the nation, if not the only one, that can oversee the management of a nonperforming asset from its primary evaluation to its ultimate disposition, *including* the completion of all proposed buildings, the finished landscaping, and the marketing and sale of the individual units.

In other words, the company provides information, advice, and actualization. "Our purpose," says Udell, "is to revitalize and manage distressed realty loans and problem properties until an acceptable disposition can take place—all the while minimizing risks and costs."

In addition to lending institutions and the specialized branches of national relocation firms, some real estate brokers are also currently hiring asset managers. But the prospective employer with the most jobs and the biggest inventory is the federal government. Because of the S&L bailout and the subsequent government insurance support of failed or failing commercial banks, Uncle Sam now holds the title of largest real estate owner in the world.

Established by Congress in 1989, the Resolution Trust Corporation is in charge of disposing of these REOs, most of them from the holdings of failed savings banks and S&L institutions. At the end of 1992, the RTC's inventory exceeded 27,000 pieces of real estate. The Federal Deposit Insurance Corporation (FDIC), which handles the problems of commercial banks, was holding more than 13,000 pieces of real estate as the year closed. Both agencies were using asset management firms to handle their properties.

To work for the government, an asset management firm must bid competitively for the contract and then sign and agree to comply with the Standard Asset Management and Disposition Agreement (SAMDA) mandated by the government. The work, however, is virtually identical to that in the private sector.

Robert Hampton of Crown Revenue Service in Columbus,

Ohio, says, "We advise the RTC on how to get the best return in the least possible time. We analyze the property, do market appraisals, and make recommendations as to the best method of disposition. When appropriate, we hire the auction firm or the real estate broker. We also hire and supervise property managers when that's necessary."

Although a college degree with a major in finance might help you land a job in asset management, most people enter the field with backgrounds in banking, appraisal, real estate sales, relocation management, property management, or land development. The work requires in-depth knowledge of all facets of real estate and well-developed communication skills plus a spectrum of personality traits that includes careful attention to detail, honesty, a cool temperament, creativity, patience, assertiveness, foresight, and perseverance. Earnings are usually salaried and commensurate with job title and responsibilities, which can range from project manager to president and CEO.

Right now, the field of asset management for lending institutions is growing exponentially, but will that last? It's hard to tell. As the economy improves, the number of REOs being held by lenders will probably decrease, and with that change in inventory, the need for asset managers is likely to diminish. The opportunities in industries other than lending look positive, however, as companies pay closer attention to cost containment and efficient management.

A number of professional associations offer publications, education, and professional designations. They include the following: the American Society of Asset Managers (ASAM), the Building Owners and Managers Association International (BOMA), and the Institute of Real Estate Management (IREM). Addresses are listed in Appendix I.

## For More Information

IREM offers a free booklet titled *Careers in Real Estate Management*. College students can also take advantage of a special offering through IREM's Institute of Real Estate Management Foundation, which now sponsors an intern program for students interested in careers in real estate management. IREM's address and phone number are given in Appendix I.

# CHAPTER 13 | Real Estate Counseling

Problems, problems, problems. Those in the land and buildings business are often faced with difficult decisions to make. Or perhaps the decisions wouldn't be hard at all if the necessary information were on hand to move in one direction or another. Realty people can turn to colleagues, to their lawyers or accountants or architects, or to any number of other sources for help with the real posers.

Or they can ask the pros. Increasingly these days they are doing just that—seeking help from professional real estate counselors.

Counselors of Real Estate (CRE), the former American Society of Real Estate Counselors (ASREC), has been in existence since 1953. It is an affiliate of the huge National Association of Realtors, and its members hold the CRE designation. In the last several years, the group has grown to 1,000 members, not a large number compared to other career specialities, but that, say those in the profession, is changing. Members are eager to bring counseling services to the attention of the public and become a more visible presence on the real estate landscape.

"Right now we're at the stage where appraising was in the mid-1950s," says Jean Felts, 1993 president of CRE. "Appraising wasn't something you made a living at back then. It was a sideline to a mortgage or real estate office or a financial institution. Counseling is at that springboard position now. In the present real estate climate, because of slow economic growth, corporate downsizing, and new regulations, more and more of those in and outside the field realize they need help. I think the next ten years are going to see a sizable increase in the demand for counseling services."

What sorts of requests can be made of realty counselors? In his book, *Real Estate Counseling in a Plain Brown Wrapper*, Jared Shlaes notes that real estate professionals—not to mention the general public—can bring counselors a wide variety of questions. Here are some samples:

- What is the best use of this property?
- Can I improve the property's performance?
- Should the property be left as is, rehabilitated, or sold?
- Would it pay to subdivide the property before putting it up for sale?
- How should the marketing people be selected and instructed?
- Would a trade make better sense?
- Who are the likely buyers?
- What kinds of financing are available?
- How long should it take to sell?
- How should I deal with toxic substance problems?
- What can I do to make the property more attractive?
- Should I rezone now or let the buyer do it?
- What are the chances of success for a development?
- How should I plan this development project?
- Is the project economically feasible?
- How will the project affect the community?
- What are the risks?
- Where should I locate my new stores?
- Should I buy, build, or lease?
- How much should I expect to pay?
- What should I try to accomplish in the negotiations?
- Can I improve the design of my real estate portfolio?
- What would be a fair way to divide my portfolio with my partners?
- How should we instruct the appraisers?

As you can see from the list, this is not a field for the novice who has only recently secured a real estate license. In advising clients, you must know your field very well indeed, although you do not have to specialize in any one aspect of real estate. The generalist is welcome here.

"It's not narrowed down," Felts concedes. "Even in most large cities, there isn't the opportunity for a counselor to specialize in one particular area. An exception is hotels, but those individuals have a national practice." Felts is senior vice-president of Dupree, Felts and Young, a commercial appraising company in New Orleans. Although most of her work is in appraising, her background—some 40 years in real estate—includes experience in construction and property management as well.

"Counseling is a facet of my practice," Felt notes, raising another point about counseling: It is almost always a part-time position, a sideline of the real estate person's principal area of focus—and income.

Most counselors are self-employed. Some accounting firms and financial institutions may hire young people straight from college, with degrees in economics or real estate, to conduct studies; these folks are, of course, salaried. A few corporations, including accounting firms, hire experienced counselors for specialized positions. In the main, however, this is a field for self-starters who expect to be in business for themselves.

Let's say you know your field. You have been in business for a while, perhaps many years. Could you start a sideline counseling service? Felts thinks you probably already have one—and are not getting paid for it! "Many people in residential sales are doing counseling and not charging for it," she explains. "Very often advice is offered in trying to secure a listing, and if there is a transaction you get paid. In my counseling practice, people need advice who are not necessarily in the market for a transaction."

How do you get started in real estate counseling? The CRE president suggests that you begin "by charging people for what you've been giving away." Felts advises,

> If somebody says, "My mother just died and a member of our family wants to live in her house, but only for three years, and we need to know . . ." You say, "Yes, I can help you, but in order to give you the benefit of my experience, I will have to charge you a fee." You also tell people, "I am available to assist you even though you may not be ready to buy or sell right now, but it will cost you some money."
>
> This is a well-kept secret: People do not know advice is available. The public needs to be educated about this kind of service, and that's what we're trying to do with CRE. Real

estate practitioners have really been taken advantage of when it comes to giving advice to the public. But they are giving away the one thing they have a limited supply of, and that is time.

Professional advising requires more on the counselor's part than merely telling the client, "You know what I think? Sell." The true counselor—and the field is not yet regulated, so anyone can hang out a shingle—does extensive research into each request, subscribes to the code of ethics set out by the CRE, and does not offer off-the-cuff opinions.

Felts describes a project she recently completed: "I analyzed a business park for an institutional client. They wanted to know how much resistance there might be to the underlying deed restrictions on the property. They were looking for a document for strategic planning purposes. I was able to provide them with information to give them a basis for their marketing plan over the next three to five years."

Is there anyone who should not try for a sideline counseling practice? Those who are not detail-oriented should avoid this career option because it usually calls for a good deal of research by the counselor. Those who should do quite well in counseling *are* interested in the fine points of questions asked them and in doing extensive work to arrive at the most knowledgeable, comprehensive answers and solutions. Those responses can be feasibility studies, market analyses, highest and best use studies, site location studies, development plans, and portfolio analyses, among other more extensive requests of clients.

Reading is also vitally important to the successful counselor. You must know your areas of expertise, your locale, and budding trends.

You can segue into counseling from virtually any real estate arena. Wherever there are people wanting answers to questions, there will be a need for a pro to assist them.

Advertising your services is not a viable way to market yourself. Most of your clients will come from word of mouth or will perhaps find your listing in a professional association directory. As you develop contacts in the field, more and more people will come to you for advice.

Income from real estate counseling is difficult to predict. This is, after all, a part-time career, and almost all members of the profession are self-employed. Still, Felts estimates that most CREs who are at the top of their profession have an income of $100,000 per year, including both their "regular" job and counseling.

Does this sound like a career option that might work well for you? Then rein in your desire to be helpful to clients and would-be clients for no fee at all and start charging for the storehouse of knowledge you have acquired in the field you know best.

## For More Information

*Real Estate Counseling in a Plain Brown Wrapper*, by Jared Shlaes, CRE, is available for $19 (no shipping charge) from the CRE. (See Appendix I for the address.)

# Urban and Regional Planning

Do you consider your city . . . a mess? Overcrowded, and traffic-clogged, and what about that area on the north side where dangerous pollutants were found?

Who solves these problems? Who designs communities to avoid them in the first place? Urban and regional planners do. We all want an efficient and environmentally sound place to call home, and that is the responsibility of these practitioners. They develop programs to provide for future growth or revitalization of urban and suburban communities and regions.

Planners' eyes are always on the future, whether that is later this month or 30 years down the road. Although perhaps guided by a vision of how things *could* be in a more perfect society, they must still work effectively with local governments, civic associations, and private business to map out the look all of those groups want for their town or county. Oh, and that look must fall within budget confines, too.

Planners take on urban revival, develop effective ways to use land and water resources, consult on new streets and highways, plan parks and other recreational amenities in a community, and, dearest to the heart of any citizen, look for ways to accommodate future growth, while keeping costs—that is, taxes—down.

It is not possible to find any one planner and say that his or her work is typical of the whole profession. Needs vary from one town to another. Dena Wild's position offers a look at one urban/ regional planner, her goals, and her occasional dissatisfactions.

Wild is senior planner in charge of community design and preservation for the city of Orlando. With the explosion in growth that her community has seen over the last 25 years, there is a need for aggressive planning. Wild notes that the city employs 11 other specialists in long-range planning, which is her department, plus planners in the city's land development and zoning departments. She is part of the growth management division, with a specialty in urban design. Wild explains, "You need a minimum of either a degree in urban design, architecture, or landscape architecture for urban design. If you don't have a master's degree, you have to have several years' experience before you are likely to be hired in this field, at least in a city as big as Orlando."

Her background includes a master's degree in urban planning from the University of Oregon, following a bachelor's degree in English from the University of Georgia.

The planner's special interest is combining the traditional neighborhood (Main Street and its accessible shops, homes, and so on) with today's suburbia with its planned communities and shopping malls. The goal is to create a large-scale, livable combination of the two. "The importance of what I am doing may take a while to be seen," Wild says, "but there are other projects I've undertaken where the results are more immediate." She mentions such short-term satisfactions as a streetscape project she was involved with; a house she designed for a city-owned site, and the saving of a dwelling of some note by seeing that it was moved to another location.

Both the past and present mayors of Orlando, she explains, have been strong advocates of planning. A pet concept of Wild's that has slowly been gathering steam across the country is the idea of sustainable communities. In these communities, everything—site planning, construction, energy—is recycled, not just aluminum cans and newspapers.

In terms of frustrations, Wild mentions the difficulty of bringing all elements of a project together, including city, developer, and citizens. "That's tough when you have to work with more than one client on a project," she explains. "When you're working in a neighborhood, you could have 300 clients, and that can be frustrating because you don't always end up with as good a product as you might have because you are satisfying so many needs. Or the project might fail entirely because of the diverse views of so many people. If you're a government planner, you'll find a negative stigma because you're associated with the government. That can be overcome, but it too can be a source of frustration."

Other planners echo Wild's sentiments, adding that dealing

with a government bureaucracy itself can cause more than a few anxious moments.

Wild's specific area of expertise is urban design. Other planners focus on land use, historic preservation, transportation, housing, economic development, the environment, and other specialties.

Many qualities go into making a good planner, but broadly speaking, these are considered the most important: (1) a capacity to analyze difficult problems and come up with imaginative ways of dealing with them; (2) a commitment to social and environmental change—in other words, not holding on to the old order; (3) a desire to work with people to help them develop their preferred solutions to the problems that concern them, for planners do not automatically know what people want; and (4) plenty of initiative.

Karen Finucan, a spokeswoman for the Washington, D.C.–based American Planning Association (APA), notes other valuable traits: "You very definitely need verbal and other communications skills. Planners these days are in the community and must be able to speak to the community. They need political know-how and savvy, too, because they are dealing with decision-makers all the time, trying to satisfy both the politicians and the citizens."

As an urban/regional planner, you will put in a traditional workweek, with most of your time spent in an office. Increasingly these days, planners are also out at sites under discussion or attending or speaking at evening public hearings and citizens group meetings.

Pay scales in the profession run quite a gamut. The APA, which represents 28,000 planners (there are 40,000 to 50,000 nationwide), elected and appointed officials, and citizens concerned with planning issues, found some gains and some losses in a 1991 survey (to be updated in 1994) the group conducted. That report showed that some 70 percent of planners work for a public agency; the remainder work in the private sector. The public sector numbers grew from 1985 figures, while the private sector numbers declined. The association attributes that decline to the recession of the late 1980s.

The public sector includes planners who work for joint city/county agencies, metropolitan or regional councils, and state, federal, and economic development agencies. The private sector takes in development and architectural offices, law firms, non-profit agencies, independent consultants, and planners who teach in colleges and universities.

The same APA report showed that the median gross salary for planners as of October 1, 1991, was $42,000. This figure represented an increase of 6.3 percent from 1989. The median entry-level salary in 1991 was $25,500, up 2 percent from 1989.

Overall, salary breakdowns looked like this, from the 99 percent who responded: 9 percent earned $74,000 or more per year; 26 percent, $50,000 to 75,000; 22 percent, $40,000 to 49,000; 26 percent, $30,000 to 39,000; 14 percent, $20,000 to 29,000; and 2 percent, $20,000.

The factors that help determine actual salaries include the planner's educational background (this factor has a great effect on salary, the survey found), the state in which the planner practices, his or her age and length of experience, the size of office, and the number of employees supervised. The survey found that planners who work for consulting firms or in private business received the highest salaries.

Finucan says, "The recession of the late 1980s and early 90s didn't take its toll on us as much as we thought. In the Northeast, yes. Florida and New Jersey are leading the way, planning-wise, across the country. California is not, in terms of ordering various types of planning. We've seen a lot of legislation lately that mandates planning, and we anticipate a good deal more with this administration. The outlook now is brighter than it was on the county and regional level two years ago, although it won't necessarily improve dramatically at the municipal level."

Planning is not a career that one can easily segue into from another real estate specialty. Although some planning agencies employ people with other educational backgrounds, ranging from landscape architecture to public administration, many others require professional planning degrees for entry-level positions and certainly for professional advancement.

Finucan says she has noticed more mid-life career moves into planning or segues into that profession from other somewhat allied careers. "Generally, people getting their master's degree in planning tend to be older than the early 20s," she points out. What Finucan is talking about here, however, is people with backgrounds in political science, government, or environmental studies. Have property managers or residential salespeople moved into planning? Not that she has noticed, she says. She pauses for a moment and then adds that when she and her husband purchased a house in the Washington, D.C., metropolitan area, there was a clause in the contract that she found particularly interesting. "We were asked if we wanted to waive our right to review the master plan for the county," she recalled. "We did check the waiver box—we already knew what was in the plan. But the gist of that part of the contract was that you had a right to see the plan before buying. If you didn't want to see it, you checked off the waiver box. It struck me how many different areas—home buying and planning, for example—are related in this real estate field."

Through its American Institute of Certified Planners, the APA offers the AICP professional designation. It is awarded after the candidate fulfills association requirements.

Several colleges and universities offer planning programs at the undergraduate and graduate levels.

## For More Information

The APA offers a raft of printed material for anyone interested in the field and for those already employed as planners. The Urban Land Institute is also a valuable source of reference materials for this profession. Broadly speaking, the ULI concerns itself with the use of land in order to enhance the overall environment. Addresses are given in Appendix I.

# CHAPTER 15 | Commercial Leasing and Sales

Who can sell and lease office buildings, office space, strip malls, retail stores, apartment buildings, warehouses, and manufacturing plants? By law, anyone with a real estate license can. In the real world, however, a highly trained specialist is invariably called for.

Part of the vast majority less than three decades ago, today the independent broker who runs a residential agency and dabbles in a few commercial transactions is in the diminishing minority. Commercial real estate is where the big deals are, and (as the night follows the day) it's where the big brokers are too. Many, like Cushman & Wakefield, have multiple offices across the United States. Some even work in the international marketplace.

Is this for you? Well, if you like working deals where all the price tags seem to have seven or more digits and if you have both patience and perseverance, you might begin to focus in on whatever kind of commercial real estate activity interests you most. Like doctors, agents in commercial real estate tend to specialize. Also like doctors, it takes quite a while before they really begin to make a good living. But the potential for riches is definitely there. Earnings of $100,000 a year are common; for a top agent in a fast market, $1 million (or more) in a single year is certainly possible.

The only problem is getting from your first day on the job to your first paycheck. Your earnings in this field are strictly from commissions. You will make nothing, no matter how hard you work, until you have a deal completed. And "completed" means when the ink is dry on every signature required at the closing table.

According to Ronald M. Mahr, a member of the National Board of Directors of the Society of Industrial and Office Realtors, a commercial deal is a decision-making process. Most take at least eight or nine months to put together, some much longer, and many tentative sales fall apart in the process.

If you add to this tenuous complexity the fact that the rookie agent must survive through both training time and network-building time, you come out pretty certain that commercial real estate sales and leasing is a career with high motivation requirements. (And, we might add, beans for dinner—a lot and for a lot of years—while you build your business and your reputation.)

If a new agent makes a deal in the first 18 months, it usually means that he or she is on the fast track. To give you an example, the *RE/MAX Times*, the franchise newspaper, celebrated the accomplishments of Steve Williams. When Williams joined his Georgia office in 1985, he was advised to expect two to three years before making his first deal. Against all odds, he closed a major transaction in seven months. That year, he won his office's Rookie of the Year award. By 1992, Steve Williams was the number three commercial specialist in the 32,000-member RE/MAX franchise.

Williams brought to his new job degrees in business and law from Indiana University and an MBA in finance from Ohio State. This preparation is, however, the exception rather than the rule among commercial real estate agents. The schooling and experience brought to this work seem to be almost as varied as the nature of business itself.

Except for each state's real estate licensing requirements, there are no education or training prerequisites mandated by law or carved in stone. Most of the learning comes after your start. Each person does seem to need a focus or specialization, however. In fact, it's often a well-developed focus, combined with high motivation, that actually lands the job. For example, some agents move into development land sales after time spent selling residential properties. Sometimes, an administrative assistant, or a salesperson, or even a person working in design or fulfillment in retail business or manufacturing will see an opportunity, get a real estate license, and move into commercial work. Some young people major in business or real estate while in college and apply to work in a commercial real estate firm right after their senior year. Some more experienced people start in their 40s or even later, after well-developed careers (and with well-established networks) in other fields.

Ron Mahr, who is also president of a large commercial brokerage firm in New Jersey, has his applicants tested by a vocational testing agency. Those that fit the profile for the job (and a few that don't but seem promising anyway) are teamed with a training agent. "It's usually three to five years before they make enough money to provide themselves even the bare necessities," says Mahr. How do they manage? "Someone helps. Sometimes it's a wife or husband, sometimes mom and dad," he continues. "It's a tough time, but those that make it reap the rewards."

Most agents interviewed agreed that specialization was a major factor in their success. But specialization has a lot of meanings in this field. For some, it means a geographic focus, which often defines the type of business they do. Carol Nelson and Mary Ann Tighe, for example, are top commercial brokers in Manhattan. That location spells a specialization in office leasing.

In less urbanized locations, an agent might work in a much wider geographical area, perhaps even an entire state, and might specialize in a broad type of transaction. Besides office leasing, some other popular specialties include office/industrial sales, investment property sales, and retail sales and leasing. Within these specialties, some agents are even more focused. Williams of RE/MAX specializes in 100- to 500-unit apartment buildings. John C. Kapas of Weichert Commercial specializes in restaurants and hotels.

Land is so important to commercial agents that there are specialties within this specialty. Many larger real estate brokerage firms have offices dedicated exclusively to land sales. But "land" in commercial real estate doesn't mean individual building lots or an occasional working farm (although there are brokers who specialize in farm sales). It usually means large tracts suitable for some kind of development.

One type of land broker is always on the lookout for acreage that might appeal to residential developers. The work of finding, listing, and selling such land includes time spent on zoning ordinances and environmental concerns. It also requires the agent to keep current on the problems, needs, goals, and advantages of area communities.

Many avant-garde land specialty offices include a staff of researchers and demographic specialists who can advise a prospective purchaser on the type of housing units most suitable to the land in question and most likely to sell in the given area. After extensive market research, they also suggest a selection of amenities that would make those units more attractive to typical buyers in the area. These specialized land brokerage offices might also provide a developer with guidance through the process of getting subdivision approval. Some of them also handle the listing and marketing of the individual units once the development is completed.

Agents who specialize in finding building sites for retail, office, and industrial developments are even more committed to researching demographics, economics, and land-use law. Putting together the deal for a shopping mall might take years. The bonus, however, is that the broker who arranges the land acquisition often also handles the leasing of its retail outlets. This means a lot of zeros in the number for the total commission earned.

Site finding for retail chains and franchises is another land broker specialty. A recent newsletter from a major commercial brokerage firm included photos of sales agents who had worked as site finders for McDonald's, Quaker Oats, Fayva Shoes, Domino's Pizza, Roy Rogers–Hardees, Kentucky Fried Chicken, Midas Mufflers, Shell Oil, and AT&T.

Although it isn't actually real estate, some commercial agents also handle business sales. Let's say a pharmacy leases space in a small strip mall. The owner might choose to sell the business, the fixtures, and the stock through a broker who will also arrange for the new owner to take over the lease on a sublet basis.

Besides the need to specialize and the extremely long time required to bring most deals to the closing table, inventory management is often another stumbling block to success in this field. By "inventory," brokers mean listings, properties for sale or lease. In the commercial arena, there is no MLS (Multiple Listing Service) and knowing what's for sale puts demands on an agent's time. Most firms do run printouts of their listings for distribution among in-house agents. However, those listed properties represent only a fraction of the potential business at any given moment because many commercial deals are still made on open listings.

In an open listing, the seller agrees to pay the broker a commission for selling or leasing the property, but the seller reserves the right to sell or lease the property himself or to sell through another broker. So it's a free-for-all, and whoever gets there first with a ready, willing, and able customer who actually makes it to the closing table gets the full commission. Needless to say, this is a career where the atmosphere is rife with competition.

Inventory management for the commercial agent therefore means not only being aware of what your agency has for sale, but also finding out what else is available or might be available if the right buyer at the right price should appear. A top agent will keep an up-to-date tickler file of "maybes" and will follow up regularly.

In addition to knowing *what's* available, you as a commercial agent, will also have to keep careful records on the specifics of each property that you are working with or hope to work with. What specifics? First, of course, the location and type of property and the name, address, and phone number of the owner or owners. Then, and almost equally important, you'll need a description of the facilities, often including photos and always including such items as taxes, square footage, building construction, electrical capacity, waste disposal, and lease terms. In short, the job demands drive, determination, extensive record keeping, and a real commitment to accuracy and detail.

Commercial real estate sales and leasing also makes extremely high demands in the personal interaction category. To be successful, you must keep in contact with business owners, residential real estate agents who might give you leads, land owners, and investors. You must be able to speak enthusiastically while still presenting all the facts. If you make a promise to do something, you must do it, and not be late. Your attitude must be positive, and your demeanor professional. The agent who loses his or her temper usually loses the deal.

You may be surprised to see that we list creativity as another requisite personality trait for the commercial agent. Most commercial deals are so full of possibilities and impossibilities that only the most creative people can see through to solutions that all the parties involved will find acceptable. An essential aspect of this creativity is the refusal to take no for an answer. When top agents hear, "It can't be done" or "It won't work," they get busy trying to prove those statements wrong.

But creativity needs bedrock. In fact, the more creative a vision is, the stronger the foundation needed to support it. In commercial real estate, that bedrock is composed of the ability to crunch the numbers, analyze the legal issues, and evaluate the pressures of economic and demographic factors. Top commercial agents integrate hard facts with intangible visions and . . .

And they negotiate! No other single skill is more valuable. Now, the mid-1990s, businesses everywhere are giving occupancy costs careful attention as part of the effort to operate lean and mean. "Careful attention" means endless demands for price concessions or space customizing before signing a lease, lowball figures on first offers to buy, and long periods of no response while negotiating. On the other hand, building owners are either thrashing to stay above water or are fighting to eke out a profitable sale. The commercial agent must bring two adamant, recalcitrant parties to a meeting of the minds. It usually takes months.

Can you learn such negotiating skills? It's debatable. One school of thought holds that all great negotiators are born that way. (Perhaps you know of one who knew the 15-minute intervals on the bedtime clock by the age of two!) But there's also a large and credible group of professionals who believe that negotiating, along with the other necessary skills of the career, *can* be learned. They are strong advocates of the certificate programs offered by the professional associations in the field.

The Commercial-Investment Real Estate Council (a subgroup of the National Association of Realtors) offers the Certified Commercial Investment Member (CCIM) designation. The Society of Industrial and Office Realtors (also a part of NAR) offers the SIOR membership designation. Both programs require proof of competence and the completion of extensive course work. The CCIM designation has sometimes been referred to as realty's PhD. Ron Mahr says the SIOR designation in commercial real estate is the equivalent of the CPA in accounting.

## For More Information

Two books from the Real Estate Education Company (a division of Dearborn Financial Publishing) may be of help to those looking for inside information on this career:

*Successful Leasing and Selling of Retail Property*, developed by the Real Estate Education Company in cooperation with Grubb & Ellis Company (Chicago: Real Estate Education Company, 1989).

*Winning in Commercial Real Estate Sales*, by Thomas Arthur Smith (Chicago: Real Estate Education Company, 1990).

To order or for a list of other titles, call (800) 437-9002, extension 650, or write to the Real Estate Education Company, 520 N. Dearborn St., Chicago, IL 60610-4354.

# Real Estate Appraisal

When you're paid for your opinion, you've got to be good. You've got to know all the formulas and procedures. You've got to know all the influential factors. And then you've got to know the could be's and the might be's. As one who gives an opinion on property values, you must be intimately acquainted with real estate sales procedures and statistics, real estate financing, real estate taxation, real estate zoning, real estate law, construction prices and practices, and local business, politics, and demographics. No wonder so few people decide to be an appraiser. You have to work your way in.

Some college students enter the field after doing part-time work gathering data for working appraisers. The most common route in, however, is through real estate sales or banking experience. In fact, until the past decade, most brokers also did appraisals on the side, and many bank executives routinely doubled as review appraisers. But the errors, market manipulations, and fraud that prompted the demise of the S&Ls have stimulated a restructuring of the appraisal industry.

"Why? What's the connection?" you ask.

It's a matter of money. Appraisers estimate property value. In most cases, the amount of financing available on a given purchase is determined by the appraised value of the property. In good times, when real estate values are climbing, everyone wants appraisals done "on the high side" because lenders have more money to lend and borrowers want to take maximum advantage of potential appreciation with minimum down payment. When the market is stagnant or falling, however, lenders get conservative and want low appraisals.

The appraiser, who is usually well aware of the preferences of the buyer or lender, must assign a value to a piece of property. And that's how the appraisal industry got into trouble. Both in good times and in bad, it's difficult *not* to serve the needs of the person or company that pays for your opinion.

In a *New York Times* article on February 23, 1992, Peter S. Brooks, a member of the firm of Austrian Roth & Partners and at that time president of the Metropolitan New York chapter of the Appraisal Institute, commented on the dilemma: "In the 80s everyone wanted high values, and now everyone wants low values. There's rarely a time when a guy says, 'Just give me an appraisal and whatever it is I'll be happy.'"

This kind of pressure and the lack of national minimal licensing standards for appraisers contributed to the banking disasters of the late 1980s. William Campbell, president and CEO of Pamrapo Savings Bank in Bayonne, New Jersey, says that there "was clearly fraud by certain segments in the appraisal industry. Federal investigations found that many bad loans were based on appraisals that were 'made as instructed'—not based on the real worth of the property or project."

"When these bad loans dragged down the S&Ls and banks that made them," Campbell continues, "they cost the American taxpayers millions and rightly prompted congressional demands that the appraisal industry be cleaned up."

As a result of the investigations, the requirements for entering this career have gotten a lot tougher. The U.S. Congress passed a law requiring that, as of January 1, 1993, each state have licensing requirements that meet federal standards. The standards include a test, certain educational courses, some on-the-job experience, and compliance with professional and ethical tenets enforced by the states. To eliminate any possibility of getting around this licensing law, Title XI of the Financial Institutions Reform, Recovery and Enforcement Act (FIRREA) requires that all federally related real estate transactions must have an appraisal performed by a state-licensed or certified appraiser using federally mandated appraisal standards. Because most lending institutions have regulation or insurance through Uncle Sam, this means virtual control.

In 1989, Congress also set up the Appraisal Foundation, a group that includes eight appraisal professional associations, to set standards for the industry and to monitor compliance. Two trade groups, the National Association of Real Estate Appraisers (NAREA) and the National Association of Review Appraisers and Mortgage Underwriters (NARAMU), have been denied membership in the Appraisal Foundation and, as of this writing, are suing the Foundation for alleged antitrust violations. So the story is not over, and the industry is not yet settled.

Despite these squabbles, the work remains the same. An appraiser estimates the market value of real property. To do this, three methods are commonly used: sales comparison (called the market data approach), capitalization of net operating income from the property (called the income approach), and replacement or reproduction costs of the property and accrued depreciation (called the cost approach).

The *market data approach* is the evaluation of the property against other similar properties that have recently been sold. Of the three appraisal methods, it is the most frequently used, and it carries the most weight in single-family residential appraisals. The appraiser uses information on recent sales available through the local Multiple Listing Service and combines it with knowledge of the community to predict the probable meeting-of-the-minds price between a ready, willing, and able buyer and a ready, willing, and able seller.

The *income approach* is the primary appraisal technique for most rental and commercial property. The appraiser attempts to determine the current dollar value of the future flow of income that can be expected from the property. To do this, the appraiser starts by estimating gross rental income based on projected occupancy levels and rent schedules. He or she then arrives at net operating income by estimating operating expenses (including real estate taxes, expenses and payroll, and insurance) and subtracting that figure from the gross rental income. The probable remaining economic life of the property is then determined in order to estimate how long the flow of income will continue. Finally, the appraiser selects the appropriate capitalization rate to determine value. Needless to say, this approach requires an experienced craftsperson with well-honed market perception to set the right capitalization rate and keep the valuation accurate.

The *cost approach* is most often used in conjunction with one or both of the other two approaches, and it usually sets the upper limit of estimated value. In this process, the value of the land is determined. Then the reproduction costs for the building are estimated using current construction cost figures. The accrued depreciation suffered by the existing structures is then subtracted from the reproduction costs. The remainder is added to land value to come up with a replacement cost appraisal.

Before a professional appraiser can apply any appraisal method, however, there's a great deal of field work to do. When an appraiser gets an assignment, he or she usually begins by driving around the neighborhood or area. Location is still the greatest determinant of value in real estate, and the appraiser takes notes on all aspects of the location: town, neighborhood, and lot.

The inspection of buildings and improvements will include observations of exterior and interior condition, measurement of the foundation to determine square footage, and notations on amenities and market appeal. The on-site aspect of the appraisal of a single-family residence might take two hours; on-site at a commercial or industrial complex might take two weeks.

In addition to on-site time, the appraiser also spends time at municipal records offices to gather tax information and to examine the deed for restrictions, easements, or encumbrances. He or she also notes current zoning and any indications of the possibility of future zoning changes.

When appraising an income-producing property, the appraiser gathers and examines income and expense records over the course of at least the past year. Vacancy rates are noted, as are expected costs for imminent repairs. Sometimes, the appraiser also studies community demographics to help in estimating future cash flow.

Finally, the appraiser will spend time in the office to calculate, write, and document the appraisal report. This commitment may be a few hours for a residential appraisal or many weeks for a huge mixed-use commercial property.

Needless to say, the profession of appraiser requires skill with numbers, attention to detail, and excellent powers of observation. It also requires knowledge of real estate law and the social and structural factors that affect property value.

Many appraisers are self-employed, working on a free-lance basis for banks, insurance companies, investors, developers, corporations, and even private individuals who plan to sell or buy a home. They are paid set fees for each appraisal assignment, ranging from $200 on up, depending on the size and type of the property and the geographical area of the country. Fees are never set as a commission based on the value of the property because percentage fees are against the code of ethics of every major appraisal society.

Is appraising a good job? Most of the more than 60,000 licensed appraisers in the United States think so. Paul Tiso is one of them. With an office in his home in Pennsylvania, he sets his own working hours. Sometimes he finds himself out in the field on weekends and evenings, but mostly he schedules his appointments at times that are convenient for him. "My wife works in international business," he says.

> And she's out of the country a lot. So this job is great for our family. I'm there to pick up the kids at the bus stop most days, and if I can't be there, I'm in the area and can be reached on my beeper.
>
> I do my paperwork mostly at home in the evenings. With a phone, an answering machine, a fax, a computer, and a modem, I really don't need to have a downtown office. That's one of the things I like best. It's great being home, working in jeans, not having to live by someone else's schedule. I put on my suit, shirt, and tie for on-site inspections, but I've been at this so long I don't have to go around to banks looking for business anymore. They call me. And honestly, I have all the work I can handle right now.

For the self-employed appraiser, expenses include a car, a personal computer, and other office equipment. Another necessity is membership in the local Multiple Listing Service if residential appraisals are a significant part of the business. The MLS provides the comparables that are essential to market comparison work. Membership in an appraisal society has recently also become essential to success (even to survival) because certification and designations have become a factor in both pay schedules and qualification for jobs involving federal regulation.

Professional appraisers with appraisal society designations earn between $30,000 and $100,000 or more a year, depending on the area of the country where they work and the type and frequency of their assignments. Some appraisers, however, work full-time for federal, state, and local government agencies. Salaries for this work are in the $30,000 range but include benefits, such as paid vacation, paid sick leave, health insurance, life insurance, and retirement plans. Still other appraisers work full-time in business, industry, insurance, banking, and international business.

Many self-employed appraisers choose to specialize. Some appraise only single-family homes; others focus on apartment houses or perhaps commercial property. Federal regulations are now setting qualification guidelines for these various specialties. Certified general appraisers may perform work for all residential and nonresidential transactions. Certified residential appraisers may perform work on all residential transactions but are limited to transactions under $250,000 for nonresidential work. Licensed appraisers without certification may only work on residential transactions valued up to $1 million and nonresidential transactions valued up to $250,000.

Review appraisers are another group whose roles in the industry are becoming more closely defined. According to Ron Beckham, director of national affairs at the NARAMU, there was a time, not long ago, when any officer in a bank who examined appraisals and mortgage applications could call him- or herself a review appraiser.

"Today," says Beckham, "the job is becoming a specialty and gaining recognition. Review appraisers examine the reports of other appraisers to determine whether the conclusions are consistent with the data reported and other generally known information. They work for the federal government, large lending institutions, major national and international corporations, insurance companies, and sometimes private investment groups."

For some reason, appraisers seem to have created more national associations than any other real estate profession. With the advent of required licensing, some of these groups have expired, and others have merged. The Appraisal Foundation in Washington, D.C., lists the following as sponsors: American Association of Certified Appraisers, American Society of Appraisers, American Society of Farm Managers and Rural Appraisers, Appraisal Institute, International Association of Assessing Officers, International Right of Way Association, National Association of Independent Fee Appraisers, National Association of Master Appraisers, and National Society of Real Estate Appraisers.

Two other major groups—NAREA and NARAMU—share a headquarters location in Scottsdale, Arizona. All addresses are listed in Appendix I.

Each of these groups has its own professional designations, and many appraisers belong to more than one group. Therefore, theoretically at least, a really competent appraiser who liked being a member of professional organizations could list a veritable alphabet soup after his or her name. Because the designations and the groups that give them seem to keep changing, we won't take up space here to list them all. You can get designation information from each professional association by simply writing or calling and asking for it.

### For More Information

Current appraisal information that meets government education requirements can be found in *Guide to the Uniform Standards of Professional Appraisal Practice*, by William B. Rayburn and Dennis S. Tosh (Chicago: Real Estate Education Company, 1993), $19.95. It is available in local bookstores or from the Real Estate Education Company, 520 N. Dearborn St., Chicago, IL 60610-4354. The book can also be ordered by calling (800) 621-9621, extension 650.

# Writing and Public Relations

Many people who are engaged in real estate have written for trade publications and have wondered if they can parlay that ability, along with their interest and experience in the field, into a writing career. Does this sound like you?

Just as most folks now working in real estate came from other career specialties, so it often is with writing. The authors of this book, for instance, have varied backgrounds. One has newspaper experience; the other has taught English and sold residential real estate. Both are now full-time writers who specialize in real estate. They write books and magazine and newspaper articles and do a variety of writing projects for corporations and professional and trade associations. You *can* have a full-time career writing about this subject, but it is a long (very long) and difficult (very difficult) path. In addition, there are no Stephen King-like incomes here!

If writing interests you more than selling, managing, and the like, you have several choices. Some are more likely to work than others.

Most daily newspapers have real estate editors, and some have reporters whose specific beat is housing and real estate. You will need more than a way with words to break in as a full-time staff person here, though. Even small papers have a long list of applicants with graduate degrees in journalism and impressive clips of their work, all waiting in line to be hired at $15,000 a year.

Daily journalism has its own highly specialized requirements: the ability to write an *objective* news story, the nosiness to ferret out what's happening in a particular specialty, and, most important, the ability to write a story under deadline pressure.

All of this is not to say that you cannot write for newspapers, just that it will be difficult for you—whether you are 25 years old with a bachelor's degree in business administration or 45 years

159

old with 20 years experience in one real estate specialty or another—to find a position now as a reporter for a daily paper.

Most papers do take free-lance articles in their real estate,
home, or lifestyle sections, and you might be able to make an
occasional contribution for a princely $50 to $300. You should
know, however, that newspaper editors cast a very wary eye on
real estate people writing on real estate (they are suspicious of
writers who are employed in other specialties too), unless they
are offering an opinion article. They know where you are coming
from and are sure your particular bias or slant will show in your
work.

There is one long-shot writing opportunity that could work
well for you. Some editors will allow real estate specialists to
write a weekly consumer column on a free-lance basis. If you
have communications skills and a thorough knowledge of your
field—and are not boring in your coverage of that material!—you
could carve out a local niche for yourself.

As an example to spur you on, let's take a look at one major
daily newspaper: the *Miami Herald*. The *Herald*'s Home & Design
section offers these columns every Sunday: a question-and-answer feature by a local Realtor and educator; a "People in Real
Estate" column, written by a *Herald* staff writer, that covers
comings and goings in the trade in South Florida; a "Shopping
Tips" column on home construction, design, maintenance, and
so on, which is a syndicated feature by a South Florida writer
with extensive writing credits; a column on pools by a nonstaff
person with knowledge in that specialty; and a "Condo Line"
question-and-answer column by an expert in that housing style.
These are in addition to a few other regular columns on home-
related topics, such as antiques and gardening.

How can *you* pick up a bylined column? Look in your local
paper to see what is missing in its consumer coverage. Is it a
column for condominium owners in a town with plenty of con-
dos? Is it a question-and-answer feature for local readers? Write
three sample columns, keeping them to no more than 700 to 750
words each, and submit them to the paper's managing editor,
along with your résumé and a one-page cover letter marketing
yourself and the column you are suggesting. If you want to write
on a different subject each week, inserting your own opinions
and forecasts, you can do that without incurring an editor's
wrath. Just be sure to include facts in there, too, and be sure that

what you have to say applies to your local readership. Do not pontificate on the broader state of the union.

You must be certain to stress to an editor that your writing will be fair and balanced and not merely a love note to the real estate industry. Consumer news is in; "puff pieces," as they are known, are out and have been for some years.

Perhaps your paper carries a column or two by a nationally syndicated writer. That does not mean that the editor will not want a locally focused article every week. Let's take a look at those national columnists to see how a column is refined—and snapped up by papers. Many dailies carry the syndicated column written by Robert Bruss, who is an attorney. Others print Kenneth Harney's housing reports from Washington, Lew Sichelman's feature, or Ruth Ryon's column from Los Angeles, which covers celebrity home buying, selling, and remodeling. In your local paper, you might also read Ellen James Martin's column, which is written for the *Baltimore Sun* and sent out across the country through Universal Press Syndicate. Her background will help you see how difficult nabbing national space can be.

Martin is a graduate of the Columbia University School of Journalism. She returned to Columbia a few brief years after graduation, having won a fellowship to zero in on business and economics. She recalls that her later work as business and real estate editor at the *Sun* gave her a close-up look at the real estate market. "I realized there was a dearth of quality real estate writing," Martin says. "So I went back to writing at my own choosing. I decided to try a real estate column, and within a year, it became syndicated." Martin's column has a style that is different from those of Bruss, Harney, and other writers. She writes in a factual, reportorial style on topics close to the heart of the average home owner. The articles contain research done by Martin, quotes from recognized experts on the subject covered, and quotes from home owners who have experienced what is being discussed that week: for example, "should you sell your home without an agent?" or "moving when you're newly divorced."

You might want to consider writing a national column and selling it to a news syndicate that would then market the column to as many papers as possible around the country. You will need some samples here too, of course, but your focus will be national, and you will need an angle that is not currently being syndicated.

Is there anything new under the real estate sun? You will have to come up with something that is.

You might also give thought to self-syndicating—that is, sending your column around on your own to daily newspapers. They can pay anywhere from $10 to $50 for such a feature each week. Of course, the more papers you sign up for your work, the more profitable the venture becomes. *The Gale Directory of Publications and Broadcast Media*, available in most libraries, lists newspaper markets around the country.

Magazine writing alone does not make for a financially viable career (unless you sell every article you write to *Reader's Digest*, which pays very well!). If you want to write for the real estate trade publications, you can expect, in many cases, no fee. Your byline is considered adequate payment.

Books are another possibility. Here again, what you need is a salable idea, the marketing skills to sell it to an editor, and the writing ability to put it all down on paper. If no mainstream trade publisher wants to buy your book idea, you might consider self-publishing, a growing field for writers and would-be writers. Self-publishing allows you to see your book in print and gives you control over distribution. Of course, you must pay the printing expenses (normally, the publishers of trade and mass-market books pick up those expenses for you).

Valli Swerdlow, who has a background in interior design, had an idea for a booklet that she self-published: *How to Dress Your Home for Success*. "I felt it was a viable subject from the start," she recalls. "It was how to sell your home fast and profitably by using my 125 decorating and maintenance tips."

After researching the need for such a publication (there is still nothing else like it on the market), writing it, and spending $5,000 working with a printer to produce it, Swerdlow has sold the 24-page booklet to individuals and to realty and relocation offices. She would not say how many copies have been sold, but she did comment, relative to the success of the project, "We've been able to renovate our house from top to bottom."

There's another option. If you have a story to tell or an idea for a valuable consumer guide but cannot write, you can hook up with a professional writer in your area and coauthor a book. Or, if you both choose, the writer can ghostwrite the book for you. The writer can do the proposal that will be needed to sell the book, find a publisher, and, of course, write the manuscript. You will probably have to pay him or her for the proposal. Once the book is sold, how you split the advance and future royalties is up to the two of you.

There's one more possibility in the book world. With the growing importance of real estate courses at the college and university level, there is a need for good textbooks. You might investigate that as well, either writing the book yourself or with a coauthor.

The resource section at the end of this chapter lists several publications that can guide you through the writing and selling process in all of the above specialties.

Uh-uh, you say, I need a *living*, not an occasional $50 or $500 or even $5,000 check every few years. Is there anything else out there?

You might want to look into a comfortably salaried public relations position. Virtually all communities of any size have a few public relations agencies. Some are just that; others combine PR with advertising services.

Builders and developers maintain public relations departments in their company offices, and so do major real estate concerns.

Whereas journalism is balanced, public relations is very definitely slanted. You are working to see that ABC Company is known throughout your community, perhaps even around the country. And you must make sure that the company looks good—always. Writing skills are definitely involved here, especially in entry-level positions. If you have writing ability and know real estate (and possess the qualities mentioned in the next paragraphs) you may well look good to a public relations firm or the public relations department of a real estate company.

Edward Rand is vice-president of a medium-size public relations agency in the New York metropolitan area. With a background that includes a degree from the Wharton School of Finance, Rand was a corporate officer in management consulting before entering the field some 13 years ago. "You have to be a good writer," Rand says, adding that until you are well up the corporate ladder in a public relations firm, you will be expected to produce news releases, brochures, letters, feature articles, and the like on your client's behalf.

Rand added that a good public relations person "knows how to think on his or her feet and consistently comes up with ideas for what the client should do—and not do. The beginner will also have to develop article ideas and be able to place them in the local media, which means learning what editors want." Are there any personal qualities that won't work well in this field? Rand points out that the person who likes routine and does not like interruptions and the person who does not want to be out front should shun this career specialty.

When you begin working in a public relations office—unless you are brought in at the vice-president level—you will probably be given a few small accounts to work with, answering to a group manager. You will work your way through the corporate ranks, the way you would in any other profession.

The National Association of Real Estate Editors accepts both real estate writers and public relations specialists, but in different membership categories. The Public Relations Society of America is another professional association for the latter specialty.

## For More Information

*Writer's Market* is revised every year by Writer's Digest Books (Cincinnati, Ohio). It lists magazine and book publishers and newspaper syndicates and their requirements. It also has articles about the mechanics of various writing specialties to assist the neophyte.

*The Complete Guide to Self-Publishing*, by Tom and Marilyn Ross (Buena Vista, CO, 1989, with a revised edition coming out in 1994) will help you put together the book you have in mind. It is published by Writers Digest Books, and distributed through the Rosses' company, Communication Creativity. For a copy, send $18.95 plus $3 for shipping to the Rosses, P.O. Box 922, Buena Vista, CO 81211.

*How to Dress Your Home for Success*, by Valli Swerdlow, is available from Valli Advisory Group, 27 Wolcott Ave., Andover, MA 01810, for $6.95.

The American Society of Journalists and Authors maintains the Dial-a-Writer referral service which can put you in touch with a professional writer. Member writers and clients negotiate appropriate fees for each project. Director Dorothy Beach can be reached at (212) 398-1934; or write to her at American Society of Journalists and Authors, 1501 Broadway, Suite 302, New York, NY 10036.

# CHAPTER 18 | Manufactured Home Sales

You probably have some idea what manufactured homes are. They're those panelized houses, right? Modulars? Log cabins? They're all manufactured homes, aren't they? Unfortunately, it is not that simple. Although all of the above are essentially made in a factory and then shipped to a lot and assembled, there are some differences among them, not only in construction, but also in regulation by federal and state government agencies.

To keep things reasonably simple in this chapter, we will talk only about manufactured homes. There are plenty of employment opportunities in this category, and you can assume that manufacturers of and dealers in different versions of factory-built houses—log and dome homes—operate pretty much the same when it comes to their sales force and hiring practices.

So, what is a manufactured home? It is a single-family house that arrives at the building site on a chassis (wheels, axle, and hitches). It must adhere to the standards of a federal code set by the U.S. Department of Housing and Urban Development (HUD).

The term *mobile home* is not used for new manufactured homes. That expression began to fall out of favor around 1976, when the HUD code was enacted. Homes of any style built after that year are called manufactured homes, and those built before are mobile homes. In 1980, the U.S. Congress changed the term officially to *manufactured home* in all of its federal laws and publications.

You will still see some older communities that are called mobile home parks, and you might hear some folks talking about "mobiles." Those who have been around *quite* a while might even be heard to say "trailer," an abomination in the industry. Indeed, today's manufactured homes bear no resemblance to the 1940s and 50s trailers that lumbered down the road attached to old Packards. Today, fully 95 percent of manufactured homes do not move from their initial location, according to the Manufactured Housing Institute (MHI), the trade association for the industry.

Since 1980, 2.8 million of these homes have been built, a growth that is expected to continue. Manufactured homes can be less expensive than those constructed from scratch on the site, and that has been their principal attraction to developers and home buyers alike. Upscale communities boast attractive land-scaping, paved streets, and often sidewalks. This type of housing can be found in virtually every price range, too, offering economy or luxury, according to the buyer's wish list and ability to pay. When driving around any area of the country, it can sometimes be difficult to tell the community of manufactured homes from the one where homes were built on their lot from the ground up.

House-hunters can erect a manufactured home on a lot they own, or they can purchase an already built model in a manufac-tured home community. Alternatively, they might buy a home and place it in a rental park where they lease the land beneath the house. There are several architectural styles to choose from too. The buyer might even opt for a carport or garage, at an extra charge. The average price of a three-bedroom, two-bath, multisection manufactured home, loaded with amenities, is around $40,000, including set-up and installation. Larger models can carry $100,000-plus price tags. The price of the home does not include land, of course.

That is a brief description of manufactured homes. Naturally, like any other house, they have to be sold, and there are many opportunities to make a living doing just that. For the hard-working individual who brings a little extra to the job, selling manufactured homes can be a very fine living indeed.

According to the MHI, there are nearly 100 manufacturers of these homes around the United States, 40 of which are members of MHI. (A sizable organization, MHI's membership also in-cludes people who work in related fields, such as finance, insur-ance, and the like.)

Manufacturers and developments used to be pretty much con-fined to the Sun Belt states, but now they are virtually every-where. The MHI says that it has seen growth in states like Michigan and Wisconsin. If you want to sell homes, then, you might first approach a manufacturer in your region. These days, you are likely to find someone relatively nearby. As a manufacturer's representative, you will sell houses principally to dealers and parks.

"It's one of the best entry levels because you learn how they're put together before you get out to retail sales," says Bob Monroe, a successful Florida dealership owner who began his own career in manufactured housing as a manufacturer's rep.

"When you contact the company," he adds, "you might say, 'Could you give me a tour around your factory and tell me a little bit about the business? I'm interested in becoming a salesman.' If I had someone come into my place with that attitude, I'd hire him on the spot."

Incidentally, *him* is the operative word here. Although the professionals in residential real estate sales are, overwhelmingly, women, it is men who dominate this industry. That might go back to the old trailer days, when mobile homes moved a great deal and were sold almost as an addition to the buyer's automobile. In those days, or course, auto salespeople were men.

Leaving the manufacturer's level, you could check around your area for a retailer, or dealership (the terms can be used interchangeably). Owners of those facilities might sell homes of just one manufacturer, or they might prefer to carry two or three labels. Some dealers zero in on high-end homes, whereas others carry the entire price range of one manufacturer. Talk to the sales manager of the showroom. What does he or she expect from the sales force?

"All the old clichés," answers Monroe. "Attitude, enthusiasm, someone who wants to work hard and make a lot of money."

What constitutes "a lot" in this industry? Entry-level sales positions should bring a salesperson around $30,000 a year. This is sometimes in commissions-only positions, but with other employers it might be a mix of commissions and a small salary. With some seasoning and the smarts to seek out new opportunities, a sales agent's income can progress dramatically. Monroe, for example, has moved around quite a bit in his 20-plus years in the industry. With each move, he bettered his position a little or a lot. For example, he went from that initial slot at a manufacturing plant to general manager of two retail sales centers that sold mobile homes. Next he headed into the retirement parks business, where buyers purchased homes to be placed on rental land.

"When they're filled, you move on to the next location," Monroe explains of those developments. Of course, this could be a disadvantage to some of these positions: Do your job, sell homes, fill up the community, and then eventually there is nothing there left to sell! So, you must move on, perhaps to a nearby community, if there is one. If not, you will probably have to segue into another area of manufactured sales or travel to a new development that is selling houses.

Monroe was sales manager for a golf course community and then became general manager and president of a corporation that developed, owned, and ran several retirement communities in the state. Finally, he bought his own business and now has two retail locations in Florida. What is the high end in terms of income? Well, Monroe says with enthusiasm, he had a healthy-six-figure paycheck when he held the position of president for the retirement community corporation.

Of course, this master salesman has spent most of this manufactured home career in Florida, a state that has seen enormous growth over the last 20 years and one that has certainly embraced the manufactured home. Still, with the growth in this industry nationwide, a good salesperson can expect a good income in other areas of the country as well as where manufactured homes have had especially strong sales. Developers find that land is expensive nowadays, and so are necessary permits, building materials, and labor. It has become cost-effective for many of them to choose the manufactured home over the site-built one. That bodes well for the future of the industry and for those looking ahead to a long career in sales there.

The salesperson quite obviously sells homes. In this specialty, selling means following up on browsers in manufactured communities or retail facilities. Once a home is sold, the salesperson must make sure that it is ordered correctly and then is required to follow its path from the manufacturer to the "building" site. He must be certain that the home is erected properly and that hookups and installations are completed to the manufacturer's— and buyer's—satisfaction. The salesperson also works with buyers in financing their purchase. As you might expect, a lot of paperwork is involved. Whereas someone handling a resale at 100 Elm Street has no need to know the intricacies of, say, the kitchen, the manufactured home salesperson must know every detail of wallpaper selections, varieties of cabinet knobs, and, if applicable, appliances that the buyer requests—plus upgrades. The manufactured home salesperson has the added responsibility of being sure that the house is erected properly. To a great degree, the intricacies of the building process do not have to concern those selling new site-built homes, although those people do, of course, have to assist the buyer in checking on the finished product.

There are no educational requirements in this field, although a few states might call for some hours of classes for salespeople in subjects such as business law. There is also no requirement for a real estate license, unless one is selling land along with the house as a realty package. Finally, there is no national professional association for manufactured home salespeople, although the industry can assist those who wish to sell. (More about that at the end of the chapter.)

Who would not do well in this career? Obviously, those who would not likely be attracted to sales—shy folks, for example— and those who are not self-starters would do well to try another field. Everyone else, especially individuals with the special motivation that Monroe describes, might well look into this career option. It is likely to be around for quite a while.

## For More Information

The Manufacturing Housing Institute will supply prospective salespeople with a complimentary list of the 40 members of that association who are manufacturers. Remember, there are about 100 manufacturers in the United States, so you will have to do some research to locate the others.

The Buildings Systems Council of the National Association of Home Builders is happy to offer its list of members who represent modular, panelized, log, and dome home builders. The addresses for the above organizations can be found in Appendix I.

# In the Real Estate Corporation

On a cold, snowy day in the middle of February 1993, the Weichert agency sold 168 pieces of property.

Ha! you laugh. "I know that gimmick. They sold a 168-unit condominium development."

No, they sold 168 *different* pieces of property. How could that be? Well, it was a good day. But not a day for the record books, not by far. Weichert Realtors is one of the two largest independent brokers in the nation (the other is Long & Foster). Both firms—along with Coldwell Banker, which at this point in time is still owned by Sears, and the huge national franchise networks, such as Century 21, RE/MAX, The Prudential, ERA, Realty World, Help-U-Sell, and Better Homes & Gardens Realtors—are examples of the growing presence of the big-business-style corporate structure in real estate brokerage. Because of this trend, both college graduates and successful students from the school of hard knocks can look for new executive jobs.

These administrative positions, often in plush office environments, have put the real estate industry into competition with "big board" American corporations as a career objective. A key factor in the new appeal to management types is the opportunity to use specialized skills.

Whereas once upon a time (20 years ago), most real estate agencies were one-person operations in which the broker (sometimes with the help of one or two salespeople) handled houses, some land, an occasional business, and a few rentals a year, today's brokers and salespeople can choose to focus on only one aspect of the business and then work with a team of expert support people. Large corporate real estate firms have specialized offices, each devoted to a single selling venue, such as residential sales, residential rentals, commercial leasing and sales, corporate relocation, or land development. In addition to sales jobs, there are multiple specialized management and support positions that allow individuals to contribute to the efficiency and success of the corporation in their own particular areas of excellence and expertise.

Let's look at Weichert Realtors, headquartered in Morris Plains, New Jersey, as an example. In addition to the 235 residential sales offices in eight states and the District of Columbia, companywide service divisions include appraisals, auctions, commercial (six offices), estates (two offices), historic homes, insurance, international, mortgage access (ten offices), home warranty, new homes (two offices), the real estate school (five offices), referral associates, relocation (four offices), rentals (13 offices), REO (real estate owned, foreclosures), and title (Southeastern Abstract, two offices). In each of these specialized branches and affiliated companies there are numerous management positions.

Weichert Realtors has ten regional vice-presidents, each of whom manages a geographical area. Supervising overall functions are two senior vice-presidents. At the top is president and CEO Jim Weichert, who founded the company in 1969 and leads it today, setting its direction and building and maintaining the human resources structure that supports it.

Besides the jobs in the Weichert organization that are obviously related to real estate, there are other opportunities found only in the large corporation. Weichert maintains a staff of researchers and trends analysts, legal counsel, public relations personnel, information and reporting systems experts, an advertising department, and a print shop that produces the brochures and direct-mail products that the company uses.

Before you put the book aside to write to us, we want you to know that we've anticipated your next question. It's got to be, "So how does one get into these management positions in the real estate corporation?" The answer is just about what you'd expect: working your way up and working your way in.

*Promotion within the company.* Betty Votta, whom you met in Chapter 9, first joined Weichert Relocation as a home-finding counselor, a job in which she worked directly with transferees. After one year, she moved into the position of corporate consultant, which involved marketing relocation services to client companies. Eighteen months later, she became manager of home acquisition, a position with national responsibility. Today, she is vice-president of client services. All of these promotions occurred in less than five years' time.

On the other hand, senior vice-president Philip Waddington has been with the Weichert organization since 1976. After working as a real estate salesperson and then as an office manager, he joined Jim Weichert to manage the first branch office that was opened. Over the years, he moved from position to position, always in roles that contributed to the growth and management of the company. Waddington was the 61st person to join the organization 17 years ago. Today, he is one of the handful in the elegant executive suites, and the company has more than 9,000 people.

*Demonstrated excellence outside the firm.* Frank Palestrini had worked for 13 years at Homequity through a number of positions and had established a broad-based understanding of the relocation business. He was a national account executive when he left to join Weichert Relocation in a highly specialized position handling foreclosed properties for area banks. His title today is vice-president—inventory management.

In 1988 and 1989, Peter Weisman was the top producer at Cross & Brown, a well-established commercial brokerage house. Today, he is executive vice-president at Weichert Commercial.

Entrepreneurship is yet another way into the real estate corporation. John G. Udell is an excellent example. He is president of Metland Properties Group, a wholly owned subsidiary of Weichert Realtors, and he got there with a creative proposal.

Udell worked as a real estate salesperson and then as a broker/owner of his own firm. Later, he became a principal in a land development corporation. With experience in real estate sales and residential building behind him, Udell went to Jim Weichert with a proposal for something that had not been done before. Metland Properties Group would not only evaluate and manage large, unfinished REO projects, it would also have the capability of completing the projects through every step—from obtaining title to building and landscaping and on to marketing and selling the finished individual units.

Udell had an idea and expertise, the Weichert organization had the funding and the support structure, and a successful company was born. To date, members of the staff have assisted in the development, construction, marketing, consulting and/or disposition of projects in New Jersey, New York, California, and

Washington, D.C. These projects include single-family homes, garden apartments, condominiums, a retirement community, office and retail complexes, an industrial park, laboratory facilities, and warehouse facilities.

Work in the large real estate franchising organizations is similar to that of the large multioffice firms with the exception that most of the offices within the franchises are independently owned. Century 21 Real Estate Corporation, the largest real estate sales organization in the world, was founded in California in 1971. Richard J. Loughlin, its president and CEO, sets direction for nearly 7,000 real estate offices in the United States and eight other countries around the world.

In the United States, the giant corporation is structured into seven divisions, encompassing 32 regions, with an additional 8 regions independently owned. Support from the division level includes training of salespeople, public relations, marketing, advertising, management counseling, new office establishment, research and information services, and purchasing of supplies and equipment. Other functions on the division level include accounting and franchise marketing.

Each of the divisions is headed by a divisional general manager, and each region is headed by a regional director. The regional office staff provides sales and service support to the independently owned and operated offices in their region. These broker-support functions include management and sales training, franchise marketing, quality service, and management consulting.

The international corporate headquarters in Irvine, California, provides the workplace for more than 150 management and support services personnel in a large variety of specialties. As in any large corporation, executives at Century 21 are both promoted from within the organization and hired because of demonstrated expertise. For example, one Century 21 divisional general manager worked his way up to that position from managing an independent real estate brokerage firm, to owning a Century 21 franchise, to selling the franchise and becoming a management consultant for the region in which it was located, and eventually to regional director, and then to divisional general manager.

Another Century 21 divisional general manager had no real

estate experience or training prior to joining the system. His early career was spent as an educator, which he parlayed into a role in regional services, training and educating brokers in his region. He, too, was promoted to regional director and then to divisional general manager.

Departments at Century 21 International include finance, accounting, administration, human resources, purchasing, international regional services, franchise marketing, legal services, advertising, marketing, public relations, convention planning, awards, publications, management and career development, training, referral/relocation, research, information services (business and financial systems), automation and systems support, and management of wholly owned subsidiaries, such as their third-party company, Western Relocation Management.

Most corporate-level positions (at headquarters and at divisional and regional offices) in the real estate corporation (both multioffice firms and franchise organizations) are salaried, often with profit sharing expressed in bonuses at the end of each fiscal year. Some jobs, such as franchise sales, require extensive travel, while others require more regular office hours. Because most of the positions are created to support the efforts of brokers and sales associates in the field, a service-oriented philosophy permeates the large real estate organization, requiring most employees to be flexible in terms of number of hours worked and the scheduling of those hours.

Most people in corporate management positions hold at least a bachelor's degree, and many have advanced degrees in business administration, law, or finance. However, positions are open to men and women without degrees who have extensive experience and proven skills. In either case, excellent communication skills are an absolute necessity. Other desirable qualities are time management and organization skills, a service orientation, and leadership, team building, stress management, and motivation skills.

Is the big real estate corporation the way of the future for this industry?

It's *one* of the ways, that's for sure. It probably won't eliminate the small independent broker, but it will be a major force in the industry. In 1991, the National Association of Realtors reported that the median gross income of residential brokerage firms was $223,800 and the average gross income was $745,000! Think how much money the few large firms must be making in order to create a gap of $522,000 between the median and the average. That's where the franchise corporation comes in. In the 1970s, they shook up a sleepy industry with corporate techniques and strategies. Today, they are helping many independents to challenge the large corporate firms.

## For More Information

All of the large franchise organizations and most of the larger real estate corporations have extensive materials available for interested prospective associates. You can get corporate addresses and phone numbers by calling a local office and asking for the information.

# And Then There's . . .

Looking for still more career choices? Here is a selection of six more real estate specialties.

## Environmental Inspector

The environment is hot, hot, hot these days, and now there is a career opportunity that focuses on that relatively new center of attention as it applies to real estate. "It's only been in recent years that the Environmental Protection Agency has been requiring environmental inspections in some real estate transactions," says Bart Kanzler, associate director of the Environmental Assessment Association (EAA), which was founded in 1990. "Also, the Resolution Trust Corp. requires a Phase I inspection be done on any property it sells."

Essentially, an environmental inspector affiliated with EAA conducts basic research for a lender, buyer, or seller. As Kanzler points out, in some instances federal legislation calls for some party to a transfer of property to guarantee that the land or building or complex is environmentally safe and clear.

The EAA's work is divided into Phase I and Phase II. Phase I can be conducted by anyone at all, the association says. After studying its course and passing the EAA test, an applicant is awarded the Certified Environmental Inspector (CEI) designation. After two years of work in the field as a CEI and after passing another exam, the senior in this specialty becomes a Certified Environmental Specialist (CES).

The inspector looks at a property for contaminated soil, air, or water and hazardous substances and materials used in construction and performs other checkups that could reveal problems. Looking at the property in question and at surrounding properties is just as important as looking inside buildings. Indeed, most environmental problems start outside and sometimes even off-site.

Research is the key: work that lenders, buyers, or sellers may not want to do themselves, although they would certainly have the same access to information that the inspector does. Some of the ways that inspectors secure needed data are by conducting title searches, checking with municipal fire departments, looking at building and sewer discharge permits, and plowing through county and EPA air pollution, sewer, and septic records for information on the property in question. State agencies have departments that regulate air quality, water, wastes, and the like and are also good sources of information. Utilities companies, too, usually have on file detailed records of environmental problems reported or noted in their regions.

Phase I work suffices for most residential situations. Phase II work calls for more experience in this area. It is done if a problem suggests itself, and the lender, buyer, or seller wants—or needs— more study. This is where environmental consultants/engineers or other pros might be called in to test the water, for example, or to conduct other sophisticated tests.

If you are interested in becoming a Phase I environmental inspector, you might contact the EAA. The association is marketing itself vigorously with lenders around the country. ("Some are very knowledgeable about the need for this," Kanzler says, "although smaller lenders are not so aware.") Once you secure certification from the EAA, however, you are pretty much on your own as far as lining up clients goes, although the association will offer suggestions for finding work. This can be a part-time or full-time career.

Some of the people who come into environmental inspection from allied fields are appraisers, brokers, and home inspectors, all of whom have some knowledge of what is likely to be involved in this work. "You do have to educate yourself in the area of the environment," Kanzler explains, "but we have also had people with no experience in real estate at all become inspectors."

The environmental inspector is as new on the scene as the buzz words, products, groups, and so on that have sprung up in recent years around the trendy "E" word. Will government agencies sustain interest in the environment over the long haul? Will this realty option be around as long as, well, as long as the environment itself? The years ahead, of course, will tell.

## Construction Inspector

From the S&L debacle of the late 1980s and the devastation of Hurricane Andrew in 1992 and its subsequent massive rebuilding has arisen the new specialty of construction inspector. From the first of those two catastrophes sprung the Association of Construction Inspectors (ACI), a San Francisco–based group that was formed in 1991.

In the aftermath of the S&L scandal, bank regulators began urging lenders to use independent, third-party construction inspectors. It was clear that many good loans had turned bad because lenders did not know what was happening at construction sites and were not carefully monitoring that aspect of the lending process. Although good loans were certainly made—a point that should be stressed because not every savings and loan institution sunk in the 1980s and not every loan in troubled S&Ls was a bad one—too much money in problem institutions was paid out on work not done or in projects where different (frequently inferior) materials were used from those called for in contracts.

Before the advent of construction inspectors, some lenders frequently conducted so-called drive-by inspections to determine whether a construction project they were financing was proceeding appropriately and according to an agreed-on schedule. Funds would be released for different stages of construction, based on those superficial glances at a building site. Sometimes, a contractor would phone in completion reports to the lender, and draws, or the next part of loan money, would be issued to the contractor on the basis of the call or the lender's drive-by look at the site.

This new group, whose members are Certified Construction Inspectors, conducts physical examinations of the building site for lenders, following a prescribed form. "When you have new construction or a construction loan is made," says Troy Johnson, managing director of the ACI, "you have city building officials coming out looking for code violations in areas like plumbing and electricity. But if I called for a marble floor in the house, no city inspector is going to make sure that's a marble floor. The construction inspector will."

Johnson says that the ACI has come up with a standard form for monitoring construction loans in the residential area and is working on a similar document for commercial construction, one that all lending institutions can use. All of this is designed, of course, to lessen a lender's liability in construction loans.

"What's helped us as an association and profession is that we've been able to standardize this part of the financing process," Johnson explains. The group has worked with what he calls "good lenders," taking sections of forms used by those institutions to create their inspection standard. From there they acquired a base of about 700 institutions, which became the first lender members of the association, which now numbers about 2,000 in all. Next they went out to individuals already conducting inspections in one real estate area or another and urged them to consider becoming construction inspectors too.

Who enters this field? Those who are familiar with construction do, folks who understand how draws are made and requested. Some come from the ranks of city code inspectors, and others might be appraisers. They are not so much leaving those specialties as broadening their talents because construction inspector does not have to be a full-time position, although some have made it into a full-time career. Care must be taken, of course, that those engaged in other areas of the construction and real estate world avoid a conflict of interest in taking on inspection. A handful of large lending institutions have hired inspectors as full-time employees, instead of paying them $500 or so per inspection; they consider this move more time- and perhaps cost-efficient. This calls into question the third-party, independent aspect of the inspector, of course, but the practice seems to be a very small part of the lending field at this time, and presumably the employee is at least concentrating on detailed inspections and not merely driving by properties in the lender's portfolio.

The ACI trains its inspectors, assuming they do have some background applicable to the field. "We've been asked by a couple of states now to look into registering inspectors," Johnson says. With standard forms, certification, and perhaps registration, the ACI seems to have found a need—and filled it—in its few short years of existence.

## Working with Titles

Title work is a field that offers several career choices, but it can be a confusing one, too, because job requirements and who is on staff at a title company can vary around the country. Title personnel can be employed by title companies, real estate agencies, lending institutions, mortgage companies, government agencies, and any organization involved in buying, selling, developing, or leasing vacant land or structures. Paralegals in law offices can also help with title work.

What exactly do those people do? Let's start with the title searcher. This individual gathers title information from the public records. A searcher might work directly with the records in the office of a public official—for example, a county clerk or recorder—or might be assigned to public record information in the facilities of a title company. This can include working in a company's so-called title plant, which is a collection of information regarding titles to property in one jurisdiction, usually a county.

Job requirements and hiring practices are at the discretion of the company, government agency, and so on, seeking help. Those requirements depend on the job, but it might be possible to start with relatively little experience, given good clerical or administrative aptitude and a knack for customer relations. Job experience often holds the key to advancement in the title industry.

The title examiner essentially reviews the results of the work of the searcher. He or she analyzes and evaluates information from title records in order to prove title. This information and the evaluation provide a basis for title insurance, which is often required by a lender for a mortgage loan. From the report of the examiner, title insurance is issued, which protects owners and mortgage lenders from loss due to claims arising from defective titles.

In some parts of the country, title examiners are often attorneys. Elsewhere, this is not the case. A check on customary job requirements in a particular locale will help with specifics on what type of preparation is needed to become an examiner.

Finally, we come to the insuring part of the title process. Jobs in this sector can range from underwriting to business development to administrative/clerical support. The nation's largest title firm is the Chicago Title Insurance Company, which has agents and branches all over the United States. The person engaged in this field might work for a branch of Chicago Title or for another major title company or in a local, independently owned agency.

Some states require the licensing of title personnel, such as searchers (sometimes called abstracters or agents). In general, though, requirements for these positions are determined only by employers.

"The largest title insurance market in the country is California," says Gary Garrity, vice-president for public affairs at the American Land Title Association (ALTA), which has 23,000 companies on its membership rolls.

Garrity notes that local laws and customs mean differences in the way title work is performed from one part of the country to another. For example, leaving Southern California, where examiners are often laypeople, and heading east across the country, you will find more examiners who have law degrees. In some states, particularly in the West, closings of real estate transactions are handled by an escrow agent. In some locales, these agents will work for a title company, whereas in others, a "closer" will work as an independent or for a different organization, such as a lending institution. "All of these differences weren't begun as a diabolical plan," Garrity points out. "It's just that every state went ahead with its own requirements as it passed through historical growth."

No pay studies have been conducted by ALTA. Salaries, like so much else in this field, may vary depending on the company and the locale. The need for title people can be cyclical, depending on activity in the real estate market.

It might be difficult for the newcomer to enter this field, whatever the state of the market, because knowledge of and experience in the field are valued. Still, the intrepid do break in, especially if they already have work experience with a real estate lender, broker, or attorney.

Like so many other careers in real estate, persistence and diligence—and positioning yourself next to the right people, such as those doing title research and insurance—can lead to just the position you want. Bear in mind, though, that depending on where you live, a law degree might be a necessary qualification for some career moves.

## Government Jobs

There are several opportunities for real estate–related work in government. There is more to a career with the government than what immediately comes to mind: Washington, D.C., and its programs and hirings.

Let's consider the federal level first. The Resolution Trust Corporation appears to be winding down its work of disposing of properties taken back from failed savings and loan institutions. Although it is not about to disappear tomorrow, it is unlikely that the RTC will have more than a few more years of existence.

The U.S. Department of Housing and Urban Development, which maintains regional offices around the country and has staffers handling specific programs on local level, has been cut back drastically, both in program funding and staffing over the last decade. Obviously, there are still some HUD jobs around, including personnel handling assisted-housing developments and related programs; staff people dealing with FHA-related loans; those working with programs and policies not related to the above; and information officers. Perhaps the Clinton administration will spur housing programs that could bring HUD back, if not to its energetic days of the late 1960s and 1970s, then at least to some improvement over the lackluster, sometimes scandal-plagued 1980s.

The federal government—and this applies to some extent to state, county, and municipal governments too—has been farming out some of the work it has needed over the last several years, giving assignments to consultants and other outside specialists rather than adding employees to its own payroll. Outside consultants have always been engaged by government agencies, of course, but since the tight money times of the late 1980s, their use has increased.

Government positions on the state and local levels seem more likely these days for the job-hunter who seeks the good pay and security of civil service employment, if only because there are more of these positions. Note, however, that there have been slashes in staffing during the last few years in many states at many levels.

You will have to check around your region for likely slots with a real estate slant because opportunities vary around the country. Some of these jobs are, it is true, patronage positions. Some are appointed jobs, but if you are qualified for the opening, then by all means pursue the appointment. State real estate commission members, for example, are almost all appointed by the governor of the state.

You know your community better than any broad overview of government jobs can provide. Having good credentials, aggressively going after the job you want when you see an opening (or, better yet, when you hear there is one coming up), and passing the civil service test, if required, might well find you putting your real estate background to good use in a rewarding—financially and otherwise—government position.

## Researchers and Trends Analysts

Every quarter, the National Association of Realtors publishes figures on existing single-family home sales. On the day they are released, these numbers are heard on radio stations and read in newspapers across the nation because they are a factor in determining how the economy is doing. Where do these figures come from? Someone doesn't just make them up. The information is researched by professionals.

But the National Association of Realtors is not the only place where someone interested in pure research in the real estate field can work. In fact, you may be surprised at the many job opportunities in this field. There are more than 50 academic real estate research centers in the nation, including Cornell University Department of Consumer Economics and Housing, Florida State University Homer Hoyt Center for Land Economics and Real Estate, Harvard Joint Center for Housing Studies, Massachusetts Institute of Technology Center for Real Estate, New Mexico State University Center for Real Estate and Economic Land Use Research, Rutgers University Center for Urban Policy Research, and the University of California at Berkeley Center for Real Estate and Urban Economics.

There are also more than 35 companies in the United States that do industry analysis, including such high-profile names as Arthur Andersen, Ernst & Young, Grubb & Ellis, Price Waterhouse, and Runzheimer International. The major franchise organizations—including Century 21, RE/MAX, and The Prudential—all have research departments, as do the largest corporations such as Coldwell Banker. The National Association of Home Builders and many other trade groups employ researchers or outsource their questions to specialized research firms. Other employers include special-interest groups, such as the Urban Land Institute, a number of real estate publications, consulting firms, investors and investment groups, and of course the federal government. The list could go on and on.

Real estate research can be divided into two main areas: economic and physical. Economic researchers gather data on how real estate is affecting and being affected by the overall economy. They analyze trends and needs regarding housing, mortgage money, commercial development, land use and availability, and urban renewal. Their findings affect government policies and programs as well as private-sector initiatives.

Physical researchers focus on buildings and structures, especially their efficiency, durability, and appropriateness for certain uses. A specialist in this field might, for example, study cluster housing as a consideration for the elderly.

Some researchers, both physical and economic, do not work with national statistics but focus instead on individual projects. Larger commercial real estate firms, for example, employ researchers to investigate the highest and best use of land or buildings that are listed. They might advise a developer on what type of construction is most likely to fill the needs of a given geographic area. They might also research demographics to advise a builder on which amenities would be most likely to influence sales in a marketing plan.

This career requires at least a four-year college degree. Most of its upper-level positions require extensive graduate work also. The most common undergraduate and graduate preparatory fields of study are economics, sociology, political science, law, urban geography, statistics, real estate, and business administration.

## Corporate Executive

When you hear the name Hartz Mountain, you probably think of birdseed and flea collars. If so, you may be surprised to learn that this company has a lot of its capital invested in real estate enterprises.

Gus Milano is Hartz's executive vice-president of leasing and finance. He and his staff manage the maintenance and leasing of 160 buildings with a total of 300 million square feet. Included in this inventory is Harmon Cove, a huge New Jersey outlet mall that Hartz developed and now leases to a number of famous-name retail outlets. Hartz also has holdings in other shopping centers and retail outlets and in industrial complexes. They even did some residential developments, although they are currently out of that investment field and have no plans to reenter.

In some ways, the job Milano does at Hartz is similar to that of an asset manager. In other ways, however, he functions as a leader and a problem solver. He initiates new projects, arranges their financing, and of course oversees their progress. In addition, he supervises Hartz's investment portfolio.

Not every corporation has its own real estate executives, but most of the larger ones do. Think about it: Whether you provide a service, sell something, or manufacture something, you need a place to do it. The larger the corporation, the more facilities it needs. If the company has expansion plans, site selection becomes a very important focus. If the company is downsizing, someone has to supervise disposition of its assets.

Corporate real estate executives come from diverse backgrounds. Some of them enter their companies in accounting or marketing and work their way into the management of real estate, as Milano did. He majored in accounting in college and soon after graduation, joined Hartz in the accounting department. While working his way up through the ranks of the company, he also earned a master's degree in finance. Today, at age 39, he has an executive office.

On the other hand, some corporate real estate executives are hired at the executive level. They have proven track records in property acquisitions, asset management, or finance, or they are proven leaders or problem solvers, often in areas in which the company is having particular problems.

Income in this realm of the real estate career marketplace matches title and responsibilities. A vice-president in a huge corporation who supervises thousands of people will certainly make more than a vice-president in a wholly owned subsidiary who supervises 50 people. You can plan on making $50,000 a year in even the smallest company, however, and $150,000 is not at all uncommon. In fact, a good number of executives with responsibility for real estate can and do pull down even more than that.

If you want to use real estate to get to the executive suite, you will need considerable education. A four-year college degree is essential, and graduate degrees are highly preferred. Business, accounting, and real estate are not the requisite undergraduate majors, however. They are preferred as graduate specialties after a broad general education.

A study conducted in 1991 by Ferguson Partners, a Chicago

consulting company that specializes in advising the real estate industry, showed that the real estate executives of the future will have to be capable of dealing with global issues because American corporations will probably continue to expand into the international market. Many executives will need to be bilingual or multilingual and will need an in-depth understanding of foreign cultures and economic and political issues.

Corporate executives who are real estate specialists also need all the management skills of any other executive. They must be able to choose the best support-team people and lead them effectively. They must be able to manage their own time, especially in unstructured situations like property negotiations, and they must be able to establish a structure in their departments that will help their subordinates to manage time effectively also.

In addition to price and return on the invested dollar, real estate executives must be aware of the current environmental, economic, and political issues. They must be well informed on issues pertinent to their business, and when they lack needed information, they must know where and how to get it, either by using the resources of the company or by outsourcing to expert contractors.

Finally, the real estate executive must be able to interact effectively with others in his or her corporation, both peers and subordinates, and with the many different professionals needed to make a real estate venture profitable. This list includes accountants, bankers and other lenders, attorneys, brokers, and local, state, and federal officials.

Most important, the real estate executive needs the kind of character that will take him or her through the many different demands of this job. Milano sums it up with two words. He says, "The real estate executive must be *aggressive* and *patient*. I know those seem to be mutually exclusive characteristics. But that's what you need!"

How many corporate real estate executives are there in the country? There are no census figures to tell us that, but the International Association of Corporate Real Estate Executives (NACORE) has more than 3,000 members. If you write to this trade group, they will send you a catalog of their publications. Another professional organization that might be helpful is the Industrial Development Research Council (IDRC). Both addresses are given in Appendix I.

# Professional Associations

Accredited Review Appraisers Council, Inc.
  303 W. Cypress
  P.O. Box 12528
  San Antonio, TX 78212
  Telephone: (210) 225-2897
             (800) 486-3676
       Fax: (210) 225-8450
  A professional association of review appraisers.

American Association of Certified Appraisers
  800 Compton Rd., Suite 10
  Cincinnati, OH 45231
  Telephone: (513) 729-1400
             (800) 543-2222
       Fax: (513) 729-1401
  Founded in 1976, this professional association comprises 2,000 real estate appraisers in this country, Canada, Bermuda, and Poland. It is a sponsoring organization of the Appraisal Foundation.

American Association of Housing Educators
  College of Architecture
  Texas A&M University
  College Station, TX 77843
  Telephone: (409) 845-0986
       Fax: (409) 845-4491
  This organization of educators and researchers was started in 1965 for the improvement of instruction in housing and its many related issues.

American Bankers Association
    1120 Connecticut Ave. NW
    Washington, DC 20036
    Telephone: (202) 663-5000
A professional association for America's commercial banks, this group provides legislative and regulatory support and educational information for its members.

American Construction Inspectors Association
    2275 W. Lincoln Ave., Suite B
    Anaheim, CA 92801
    Telephone: (714) 772-7590
Members of this group are both construction inspectors and home inspectors.

American Industrial Real Estate Association
    345 S. Figueroa, Suite M-1
    Los Angeles, CA 90071
    Telephone: (213) 687-8777
         Fax: (213) 687-8616
This group, concerned with industrial real estate, has a membership of more than 1,500 brokers and associates in Southern California.

American Institute of Architects
    1735 New York Ave. NW
    Washington, DC 20006
    Telephone: (202) 626-7300
         Fax: (202) 626-7421
This professional association is organized into state societies and local chapters.

American Institute of Real Estate Appraisers
    430 N. Michigan Ave.
    Chicago, IL 60611
    Telephone: (312) 329-8559
This professional association is an arm of the National Association of Realtors.

American Land Title Association (ALTA)
    1828 L St. NW, Suite 705

Washington, DC 20036
Telephone: (202) 296-3671
    Fax: (202) 223-5843
The members of this national association of the abstract and title insurance industry search, review, and insure land titles to protect home buyers, mortgage lenders, and other investors.

American Planning Association (APA)
1776 Massachusetts Ave. NW, Suite 400
Washington, DC 20036
Telephone: (202) 872-0611
This research group represents nearly 30,000 planners, elected and appointed officials, and citizens who are involved in development issues.

American Real Estate and Urban Economics Association
School of Business
Indiana University
Bloomington, IN 47405
Telephone: (812) 885-7794
This professional organization of almost 1,000 real estate researchers is employed by the government, universities, and private organizations.

American Real Estate Society
University Center, 513
James J. Nance College of Business
Cleveland State University
Cleveland, OH 44115
Telephone: (216) 687-4732
    Fax: (216) 687-9544
This organization serves as a liaison between practicing real estate professionals and academics in the field and conducts research to assist real estate practitioners. Dr. James R. Webb, the executive director, is the contact.

American Resort and Residential Development Association (ARRDA)
1220 L St. NW, Suite 510
Washington, DC 20005
Telephone: (202) 371-6700

Fax: (202) 289-8544

ARRDA's membership comprises developers of residential resort, recreational time-sharing, and recreational vehicle communities and others in that industry.

American Society of Appraisers
P.O. Box 17265
Washington, DC 20041
Telephone: (703) 478-2228
Fax: (703) 742-8471

This professional association is a sponsor of the Appraisal
Foundation.

American Society of Asset Managers (ASAM)
303 W. Cypress St.
P.O. Box 12528
San Antonio, TX 78212
Telephone: (210) 225-2897
(800) 486-3676
Fax: (210) 225-8450

An association of real property managers.

American Society of Farm Managers and Rural Appraisers
950 S. Cherry St., Suite 106
Denver, CO 80222
Telephone: (303) 758-3513
Fax: (303) 758-0190

This professional association is a sponsor of the Appraisal
Foundation.

American Society of Home Inspectors (ASHI)
85 W. Algonquin Rd.
Arlington Heights, IL 60005
Telephone: (708) 290-1919
(800) 743-ASHI
Fax: (708) 290-1920

This is the principal national organization for independent
professional home inspectors in the United States and Canada.

American Society of Professional Appraisers
1100 Abernethy Rd., Suite 625

Atlanta, GA 30328
Telephone: (404) 551-8187
This professional association for real estate appraisers was established in 1984.

Appraisal Foundation
1029 Vermont Ave. NW
Washington, DC 20005
Telephone: (202) 347-7722
    Fax: (202) 347-7727
This nonprofit educational organization, established by the appraisal profession, was created to foster professionalism in the industry. The foundation has several sponsoring national organizations in real estate appraisal specialties.

Appraisal Institute
875 N. Michigan Ave., Suite 2400
Chicago, IL 60611
Telephone: (312) 335-4100
    Fax: (312) 335-4400
This professional association of real estate appraisers, with a legislative office in Washington, D.C., is a sponsor of the Appraisal Foundation.

Association for Commercial Real Estate (NAIOP)
1215 Jefferson Davis Hgwy., Suite 100
Arlington, VA 22202
Telephone: (703) 979-3400
    Fax: (703) 979-3409
The members of NAIOP (formerly the National Association of Industrial and Office Parks) are involved in the development of industrial, office, and retail properties.

Association for Preservation Technology International
P.O. Box 8178
Fredericksburg, VA 22404
Telephone: (703) 373-1621
    Fax: (703) 373-6050
This organization is dedicated to improving professional practices in the restoration of properties more than 25 years old. Rehab advice is available.

Association of Construction Inspectors
    44 Montgomery St., Suite 500
    San Francisco, CA 94104
    Telephone: (415) 292-7575
            Fax: (415) 986-9640
A professional association for construction inspectors and others interested in the field, including lenders.

Building Owners and Managers Association (BOMA)
    1201 New York Ave. NW
    Washington, DC 20005
    Telephone: (202) 408-2662
            Fax: (202) 371-0181
BOMA is the oldest and largest trade association representing the office building industry.

Counselors of Real Estate (CRE)
    430 N. Michigan Ave.
    Chicago, IL 60611
    Telephone: (312) 329-8427
            Fax: (312) 329-8881
Formerly the American Society of Real Estate Counselors (ASREC). This professional association for those engaged in real estate counseling was renamed in 1993.

Downtown Research and Development Center
    215 Park Ave., Suite 1301
    New York, NY 10003
    Telephone: (212) 228-0246
            Fax: (212) 228-0376
This 40-year-old organization is dedicated to research and reporting on urban problems and solutions.

Employee Relocation Council
    1720 N St. NW
    Washington, DC 20036
    Telephone: (202) 857-0857
            Fax: (202) 467-4012
This 10,000-member professional organization comprises corporate and relocation service companies that are involved in employee transfers.

Environmental Assessment Association
8383 E. Evans Rd.
Scottsdale, AZ 85260
Telephone: (602) 483-8100
Fax: (602) 998-8022
This professional organization represents more than 5,000 environmental inspectors.

Hotel and Motel Brokers of America
10220 N. Executive Hills Blvd., Suite 610
Kansas City, MO 64153
Telephone: (816) 891-7070
(800) 821-5191
Fax: (816) 891-7071
Independently owned and operated real estate firms handling the sale, exchange, and syndication of hotels and motels belong to this organization.

Industrial Development Research Council
40 Technology Park/Atlanta, Suite 200
Norcross, GA 30092
Telephone: (404) 446-8955
Founded in 1961, the council is a professional association for corporate real estate and facility-planning executives.

Institute of Real Estate Management (IREM)
430 N. Michigan Ave.
Chicago, IL 60611
Telephone: (312) 661-0004
Fax: (312) 661-0217
An arm of the National Association of Realtors, IREM is the professional association for managers of all types of income-producing real estate.

International Association of Assessing Officers
1313 E. 60th St.
Chicago, IL 60637
Telephone: (312) 947-2069
Fax: (312) 383-2246
A sponsor of the Appraisal Foundation.

International Association of Corporate Real Estate Executives
(NACORE)
  440 Columbia Dr., Suite 100
  West Palm Beach, FL 33409
  Telephone: (407) 683-8111
           (800) 726-8111
       Fax: (407) 697-4853
NACORE (formerly the National Association of Corporate Real
Estate Executives) kept its original acronym when it broadened
its interests to include international real estate. It is concerned
with development and real estate asset management for major
corporations and the like, with an international focus.

International Council of Real Estate Consulting Professionals
  297 Dakota St.
  LeSueur, MN 56058
  Telephone: (612) 665-6280
Members of this group work in fields related to professional
consulting, including sales, accounting, and finance.

International Council of Shopping Centers
  665 Fifth Ave.
  New York, NY 10022
  Telephone: (212) 421-8181
       Fax: (212) 486-0849
This trade association, with 25,000 members in 42 countries,
includes owners, developers, retailers, and lenders.

International Right of Way Association
  13650 S. Gramercy Pl., Suite 100
  Gardenia, CA 90249
  Telephone: (310) 538-0233
       Fax: (310) 538-1471
A sponsoring organization of the Appraisal Foundation.

Manufactured Housing Institute (MHI)
  1745 Jefferson Davis Hgwy.
  Arlington, VA 22202
  Telephone: (703) 413-6620

This trade association comprises those who work in this industry, which includes a variety of structures made in a factory, then shipped to the building site.

Mortgage Bankers Association of America
1125 15th St. NW
Washington, DC 20005
Telephone: (202) 861-6500
Fax: (202) 861-0736
More than 2,000 mortgage companies, savings and loan associations, commercial banks, savings banks, life insurance companies, and others in the mortgage lending field belong to this trade association.

National Association of Counselors
303 W. Cypress St.
P.O. Box 12528
San Antonio, TX 78212
Telephone: (512) 225-2897
(800) 486-3676
Fax: (512) 225-8450
An organization of real estate counselors.

National Association of Home Builders
1201 15th St. NW
Washington, DC 20005
Telephone: (202) 822-0200
(800) 368-5242
With some 150,000 members, including local and state associations, NAHB represents primarily builders but also includes those in mortgage finance, architecture, contracting, and related services. Its Buildings Systems Council comprises factory-built home manufacturers.

National Association of Independent Fee Appraisers
7501 Murdoch Ave.
St. Louis, MO 63119
Telephone: (314) 781-6688
Fax: (314) 781-2872
A professional organization for real estate appraisers.

National Association of Master Appraisers
  303 W. Cypress St.
  P.O. Box 12617
  San Antonio, TX 78212
  Telephone: (512) 271-0781
              (800) 229-6262
      Fax: (512) 225-8450
  An association of real estate appraisers.

National Association of Mortgage Brokers
  706 E. Bell Rd., Suite 101
  Phoenix, AZ 85022
  Telephone: (602) 992-6181
      Fax: (602) 493-8711
  This professional association provides legislative and educational services for mortgage brokers.

National Association of Real Estate Appraisers (NAREA)
  8383 E. Evans Rd.
  Scottsdale, AZ 85260
  Telephone: (602) 948-8000
      Fax: (602) 998-8022
  This professional association for appraisers has more than 23,000 members throughout the United States.

National Association of Real Estate Editors
  3101 N. Central Ave., Suite 560
  Phoenix, AZ 85012
  Telephone: (602) 265-1699
      Fax: (602) 230-8504
  Print and broadcast journalists who are interested in all areas of real estate—housing, investment, design, finance, and so on—belong to this professional organization.

National Association of Real Estate License Law Officials
  P.O. Box 129
  Centreville, UT 84014
  Telephone: (801) 298-5572
  This association coordinates activities among state real estate boards and commissions, including the licensing of real estate professionals in the United States and parts of Canada.

National Association of Realtors (NAR)
430 N. Michigan Ave.
Chicago, IL 60611
Telephone: (312) 329-8200
Fax: (312) 329-8576
This 750,000-member organization of residential and commercial Realtors, the nation's largest trade and professional association, includes salespeople, brokers, property managers, appraisers, counselors, and others engaged in the industry. Several of the groups in this listing are affiliates of NAR.

National Association of Review Appraisers and Mortgage Underwriters (NARAMU)
8383 E. Evans Rd.
Scottsdale, AZ 85260
Telephone: (602) 998-3000
Fax: (602) 998-8022
A professional association for those specialists.

National Auctioneers Association
8880 Balentine
Overland Park, KS 66214
Telephone: (913) 541-8084
Fax: (913) 894-5281
This professional organization for auctioneers is not limited to those who specialize in real estate auctions.

National Society of Real Estate Appraisers
1265 E. 105th St.
Cleveland, OH 44108
Telephone: (216) 795-3445
Fax: (216) 721-3336
This appraisal group is a sponsoring organization of the Appraisal Institute.

Real Estate Educators Association
One Illinois Center, Suite 200
111 E. Wacker Dr.
Chicago, IL 60601
Telephone: (312) 616-0800

The members of this umbrella organization include teachers, trainers, and writers. The association has chapters in 30 states and regions and offers teaching techniques, information on materials, and so on.

Real Estate Brokerage Managers Council
  430 N. Michigan Avenue
  Chicago, IL 60611-4092
          (312) 670-3780
      Fax: (312) 329-8882
A national organization for broker office managers.

Savings and Community Bankers of America
  900 19th St. NW, Suite 400
  Washington, DC 20006
  Telephone: (202) 857-3100
      Fax: (202) 296-8716
This principal trade association for the nation's savings and community banks was formed in 1992 by a merger of the U.S. League of Savings Institutions and the National Council of Community Bankers.

Society of Industrial and Office Realtors
  777 14th St. NW, Suite 400
  Washington, DC 20005
  Telephone: (202) 737-1150
      Fax: (202) 737-3142
An international association for those who specialize in commercial and industrial real estate.

Urban Land Institute
  625 Indiana Ave. NW, Suite 400
  Washington, DC 20004
  Telephone: (202) 624-7000
      Fax: (202) 624-7140
Broadly speaking, this organization concerns itself with the use of land in order to enhance the overall environment.

# Where to Study Real Estate

Your choices in the study of real estate range from a one-day seminar held in the ballroom of a local hotel to a degree program at a college or university. The following advice will help you to pursue the courses you need to achieve a productive career in real estate.

If you are interested in becoming a real estate salesperson, contact your state real estate commission (addresses and telephone numbers can be found in Appendix III). The commission will be able to tell you where the courses required for a real estate license are offered in your state. You might also call the large realty offices in your area. Many offer free courses for prospective salespeople (adult education courses usually charge a fee). You do not have to join the realty office's sales force after you secure your license.

If you are now engaged in real estate and want to pursue certification or just brush up on a particular area of your field, contact the professional association for your career. Most sponsor workshops, seminars, and so on at different locations around the country during the year. You might be lucky enough to find one held in your city, or you might have to travel some distance to participate.

Look at catalogs for the adult schools in your area, or check out the continuing education courses offered at colleges or universities near you. You might find primer courses offered in subjects such as introductory appraising or renovating houses for profit. For a fairly low cost—usually about $25 for adult ed classes or $100 for credit classes—you can learn about the field that interests you. Without spending much time or money, you can determine whether you want to pursue that subject on a more elaborate scale, perhaps obtaining a college degree in that specialty.

If you are interested in pursuing an undergraduate or post-graduate degree in real estate, your public library can help you find the college or university that best suits your needs. Here are some publications you can request from the reference librarian. New editions come out annually or biennially:

*Barron's Profiles of American Colleges* (Barron's Education Series).

*College Board Index of Majors* (New York: College Entrance Examination Board).

*Lovejoy's College Guide* (Prentice Hall).

*Peterson's Graduate Programs in Business, Education, Health and Law* (Princeton, NJ: Peterson's Guides).

*Peterson's Guide to Four-Year Colleges* (Princeton, NJ: Peterson's Guides).

*Peterson's Guide to Two-Year Colleges* (Princeton, NJ: Peterson's Guides).

*Technical, Trade and Business School Data Handbook, Including Community and Junior Colleges* (Concord, MA: Orchard House).

The Urban Land Institute offers *The Directory of Real Estate Development and Related Education Programs,* an updated and expanded catalog of 59 university education programs in the United States, Canada, the Netherlands, and New Zealand. Each entry includes degree and degree specialization offered, program description, core curriculum, tuition, and job placement assistance. Covered in the book are undergraduate and graduate degree programs with development specialties. The book costs $15 for ULI members; $19 for nonmembers. ULI's address can be found in Appendix I.

# Directory of Real Estate License Law Officials

For information about the licensing of real estate professionals, contact the official in your area.

**Alabama**
D. Philip Lasater
Real Estate Commission
1201 Carmichael Way
Montgomery, AL 36106
(205) 242-5544

**Alaska**
Grayce A. Oakley
Division of Occupational
  Licensing
3601 C St., Suite 722
Anchorage, AK 99503
(907) 563-2169

**Alberta**
Rudolph J. Palovcik
Consumer and Corporate
  Affairs
10025 Jasper Ave., 19th Floor
Edmonton, Alberta T5J 3Z5
(403) 422-1588

**Arizona**
Jerry A. Holt
Department of Real Estate
202 E. Earll Dr. #400
Phoenix, AZ 85012
(602) 279-2909

**Arkansas**
Roy L. Bilheimer
Real Estate Commission
612 S. Summit St.
Little Rock, AR 72201-4740
(501) 682-2732

**British Columbia**
P. Dermot Murphy
Real Estate Council of British
  Columbia
750 W. Pender St., Suite 900
Vancouver, British Columbia
  V6C 2T8
(604) 683-9664

**California**
Clark Wallace
Department of Real Estate
185 Berry St., Room 3400
San Francisco, CA 94107
(415) 904-5900

**Colorado**
Michael B. Gorham
Department of Regulatory
  Agencies
Real Estate Commission
1776 Logan St., 4th Floor

Denver, CO 80203
(303) 894-2166

**Connecticut**
Laurence L. Hannafin
Department of Consumer
  Protection
Real Estate Division
165 Capitol Ave., Room G-8
Hartford, CT 06106
(203) 566-5130

**Delaware**
Dave Hill
Department of Administrative
  Services
O'Neill Building
P.O. Box 1401
Dover, DE 19902
(302) 739-4522

**District of Columbia**
Leon W. Lewis
Department of Consumer and
  Regulatory Affairs
614 H St. NW, Room 913
P.O. Box 37200
Washington, DC 20013-7200
(202) 727-7853

**Florida**
Darlene F. Keller
Department of Professional
  Regulation
Division of Real Estate
400 W. Robinson St.
Orlando, FL 32801
(407) 423-6053

**Georgia**
Charles Clark

Real Estate Commission
Sussex Place, Suite 500
148 International Blvd. NE
Atlanta, GA 30303
(404) 656-3916

**Guam**
Joaquin G. Blaz
Insurance, Securities,
  Banking, and Real Estate
  Division
855 W. Marine Dr.
Agana, GU 96910
(671) 477-5145

**Hawaii**
Calvin T. Kimura
Real Estate Commission
Department of Commerce
  and Consumer Affairs
250 S. King St., Room 702
Honolulu, HI 96813
(808) 586-2643

**Idaho**
Jeri Pyeatt
Real Estate Commission
Statehouse Mail
Boise, ID 83720
(208) 334-3285

**Illinois**
Julie A. Mategrano
Department of Professional
  Regulation
320 W. Washington St.
Springfield, IL 62786
(217) 782-7566

**Indiana**
Gerald Quigley

Professional Licensing Agency
1021 Government Center N
100 N. Senate Ave.
Indianapolis, IN 46204
(317) 232-2980

**Iowa**
Roger L. Hansen
Professional Licensing and
  Regulation Division
Real Estate Commission
1918 S.E. Hulsizer Ave.
Ankeny, IA 50021
(515) 281-3183

**Kansas**
E. W. Yockers
Real Estate Commission
Landon State Office Building
900 Jackson St., Room 501
Topeka, KS 66612
(913) 296-3411

**Kentucky**
W. Chris Alford
Real Estate Commission
10200 Linn Station Rd., Suite
  201
Louisville, KY 40223
(502) 425-4273

**Louisiana**
J. C. Willie
Real Estate Commission
P.O. Box 14785
Baton Rouge, LA 70898-4785
(504) 925-4771

**Maine**
Carol J. Leighton
Real Estate Commission

State House Station #35
Augusta, ME 04333
(207) 582-8727

**Maryland**
Elizabeth A. Beggs
Real Estate Commission
501 St. Paul Place, 8th Floor
Baltimore, MD 21202
(410) 333-6230

**Massachusetts**
Joseph R. Autilio
Board of Registration of Real
  Estate Brokers and
  Salesmen
Real Estate Board
100 Cambridge St., Room 1518
Boston, MA 02202
(617) 727-2373

**Michigan**
Ann Millben
Department of Commerce
BOPR—Office of Commercial
  Services
Licensing Division
P.O. Box 30243
Lansing, MI 48909
(517) 373-0490

**Minnesota**
Barbara M. Lessard
Commerce Department
133 E. 7th St.
St. Paul, MN 55101
(612) 296-2488

**Mississippi**
John W. Neeley
Real Estate Commission

1920 Dunbarton Dr.
Jackson, MS 39216
(601) 987-3969

**Missouri**
Janet Brandt Thomas
Real Estate Commission
P.O. Box 1339
Jefferson City, MO 65102
(314) 751-2628

**Montana**
Grace A. Berger
Department of Commerce
Board of Realty Regulation
111 N. Jackson
Helena, MT 59620
(406) 444-2961

**Nebraska**
Les Tyrrell
Real Estate Commission
301 Centennial Mall S
P.O. Box 94667
Lincoln, NE 68509
(402) 471-2004

**Nevada**
George W. Whitney
Real Estate Division
1665 Hot Springs Rd.
Capitol Complex
Carson City, NV 89710
(702) 687-4280

**New Brunswick**
Carl Sherwood
Real Estate Council
P.O. Box 785
Fredericton, New Brunswick
   E3B 5B4
(506) 455-9733

**New Hampshire**
John P. Cummings
Real Estate Commission
95 Pleasant St.
Spaulding Bldg.
State Office Park S
Concord, NH 03301
(603) 271-2701

**New Jersey**
Micki Greco Shillito
Real Estate Commission
20 W. State St. CN-328
Trenton, NJ 08625
(609) 292-8280

**New Mexico**
Jim Apodaca
Real Estate Commission
1650 University Blvd. NE,
   Suite 490
Albuquerque, NM 87102
(505) 841-9120

**North Carolina**
Philip T. Fisher
Real Estate Commission
P.O. Box 17100
Raleigh, NC 27619
(919) 733-9580

**North Dakota**
Dennis D. Schulz
Real Estate Commission
314 E. Thayer Ave.
P.O. Box 727
Bismarck, ND 58502
(701) 224-2749

**Ohio**
Dennis Tatum

Division of Real Estate
77 S. High St.
Columbus, OH 43266
(614) 466-4100

**Oklahoma**
Norris Price
Real Estate Commission
4040 N. Lincoln Blvd., Suite 100
Oklahoma City, OK 73105
(405) 521-3387

**Ontario**
Gordon J. Randall
Real Estate and Business
   Brokers Act
555 Yonge St., 3rd Floor
Toronto, Ontario M7A 2H6
(416) 326-8680

**Oregon**
Morella Larsen
Real Estate Agency
158 12th Street NE
Salem, OR 97310
(503) 378-4170

**Pennsylvania**
Teresa A. Woodall
Real Estate Commission
Bureau of Professional and
   Occupational Affairs
Transportation and Safety
   Bldg., Room 611
P.O. Box 2649
Harrisburg, PA 17105
(717) 783-3658

**Quebec**
Real Martel

Service du Courtage
   Immobilier du Quebec
Ministere Des Finances
220 Grande-Allee Est, Suite 910
Quebec, Quebec G1R 2J1
(418) 643-4597

**Saskatchewan**
Kirk Bacon
Real Estate Commission
3929 8th St. E, #107
Saskatoon, Saskatchewan
   S7H 5M2
(307) 374-5233

**South Carolina**
Henry L. Jolly
Real Estate Commission
1201 Main St., Suite 1500
Columbia, SC 29201
(803) 737-0700

**South Dakota**
Larry G. Lyngstad
Real Estate Commission
P.O. Box 490
Pierre, SD 57501
(605) 773-3600

**Tennessee**
Bruce E. Lynn
Real Estate Commission
500 James Robertson Pkwy.
Suite 180, Volunteer Plaza
Nashville, TN 37243
(615) 741-2273

**Texas**
Wallace Collins
Real Estate Commission
P.O. Box 12188

Austin, TX 78711
(512) 459-6544

**Utah**
Blaine E. Twitchell
Department of Commerce
Division of Real Estate
P.O. Box 45806
Salt Lake City, UT 84145
(801) 530-6747

**Vermont**
Jean E. Brown
Real Estate Commission
109 State St.
Montpelier, VT 05609
(802) 828-3228

**Virginia**
Joan L. White
Department of Commerce
3600 W. Broad St., 5th Floor
Richmond, VA 23230
(804) 367-8552

**Virgin Islands**
Marylyn A. Stapleton
Department of Licensing and
  Consumer Affairs
Bldg. #1 Subbase
Property and Procurement
  Bldg., Room 205
St. Thomas, VI 00802
(809) 774-3130

**Washington**
Sydney W. Beckett

Department of Licensing
Professional Licensing Services
Real Estate Program
P.O. Box 9015
Olympia, WA 98507
(206) 586-6101

**West Virginia**
Richard E. Strader
Real Estate Commission
1033 Quarrier St., Suite 400
Charleston, WV 25301
(304) 558-3555

**Wisconsin**
Cletus J. Hansen
Department of Regulation
  and Licensing
Bureau of Direct Licensing
  and Real Estate
1400 E. Washington Ave.,
  Room 281
P.O. Box 8935
Madison, WI 53708
(608) 267-7134

**Wyoming**
Constance K. Anderson
Real Estate Commission
205 Barrett Bldg.
Cheyenne, WY 82002
(307) 777-7141

*Source:* National Association of
Real Estate License Law Officials

# Index